D0377204

# CALLED TO COMMUNION

JOSEPH CARDINAL RATZINGER

# Called to Communion

## Understanding the Church Today

TRANSLATED BY
ADRIAN WALKER

IGNATIUS PRESS    SAN FRANCISCO

Title of the German original:
*Zur Gemeinschaft gerufen: Kirche heute verstehen*
second edition, © 1991 Herder, Freiburg im Breisgau

Cover design by Roxanne Mei Lum

Cover art: Scala /Art Resource, New York

(Left panel): Duccio. *The Last Supper* (detail)
Museo dell'Opera Metropolitana, Siena, Italy.
(Center): Cimabue. *Crucifixion* (detail)
San Domenico, Arezzo, Italy.
(Right): Duccio. *Pentecost* (detail)
Museo dell'Opera Metropolitana, Siena, Italy.

© 1996 Ignatius Press, San Francisco
All rights reserved
ISBN 0-89870-578-9
Library of Congress catalogue number 95-79953
Printed in the United States of America ∞

# Contents

# Foreword

Today the question of the Church has to a large extent become the question of how the Church can be changed and ameliorated. Yet even someone who wishes to improve upon a mechanical device, and all the more someone who wants to heal an organism, must first investigate how the apparatus is designed or how the organism is inwardly structured. If doing so is not to prove blind and thereby destructive, it must be preceded by inquiry about being. Today as always, the will to take action in regard to the Church must find the patience first to ask about her nature, her origin, her destination; today as always, ecclesial ethos can develop properly only when it allows itself to be illuminated and led by the logos of faith.

In this spirit, the five chapters of this book attempt to offer a sort of primer of Catholic ecclesiology. The first three chapters were written for a theology course in Rio de Janeiro that drew a gathering of around a hundred bishops from every quarter of Brazil between the twenty-third and the twenty-seventh of July 1990. The principal question concerned the relationship between the universal Church and the particular Church, with special regard to the primacy of the successor of Peter and its relation to the ministry of the bishops. The

brotherly atmosphere that reigned during those days together became almost without any effort of ours a concrete interpretation of the assigned topic. We were fa-
vored with a delightful experience of catholicity with
its living interplay of unity and plurality; I hope that for
its part the written word can still convey something of
the spirit in which we lived and worked together and
in this way help toward a renewed understanding of the
Church.

To these three chapters I have added the address
that I presented at the opening of the Synod of Bishops on the priesthood in October 1990 as an introduction to the synodal consultations on priestly formation.
Furthermore, my talk on the Church and ecclesial reform, which concluded the annual meeting at Rimini on
September 1, 1990, has been incorporated into this volume. These additions were meant to give the problem
of the existence and structure of the Church a needed
breadth beyond the vision of the Rio conferences, whose
horizon was defined primarily in terms of the episcopal office. At the same time, they were intended to link
this problem to contemporary questions touching the
life of the Church. It was likewise the lively public re-
action provoked by these two texts that made their inclusion in this volume seem appropriate. A homily that
I preached in January 1990 at the seminary in Philadel-
phia attempts by way of conclusion to clarify once more
the spiritual orientation of the whole book. I hope that

this small volume can bring clarity and help in the crisis of ecclesial consciousness through which we are now living.

JOSEPH CARDINAL RATZINGER

Rome, on the Feast of
the Epiphany, 1991

# I

# The Origin and Essence
# of the Church

## *1. Preliminary considerations on method*

The questions that occupy today's discussion of the
Church are mostly of a practical nature: What is the
responsibility of the bishop? What is the significance
of the particular Churches in the whole of the Church
of Jesus Christ? What is the *raison d'être* of the papacy?
How should the bishops and the pope, the particular
Church and the universal Church work together? What
is the status of the layman in the Church?[1] In order to
be able to respond correctly to these practical problems,
we must premise the fundamental question: What is the
Church in the first place? What is the purpose of her
existence? What is her origin? Did Christ actually will
her, and, if so, how did he intend her to be? Only if
we are able to reply properly to these basic questions
do we have any chance of finding an adequate answer
to the particular practical problems mentioned above.

Yet the very question about Jesus and the Church,
as well as about the initial form of the Church in the

[1] The selection of these questions, which could be extended in
multiple directions, was determined by the formulation of the themes
of the study course for which the first three chapters were written.

New Testament itself, is so overgrown by the tangled thicket of exegetical hypotheses that there is seemingly next to no hope of finding any sort of adequate answer to it. There thus exists the dangerous temptation to pick out the solutions that appear most congenial or else to skip over the problem entirely in order to plunge immediately into practical matters. But this sort of pastoral ministry would be founded upon skepticism; we would, should we adopt it, no longer be attempting to follow the Lord but would be groping about blindly toward what appeared attainable to us: we would become blind men leading the blind (cf. Mt 15:14).

A way through the primeval forest of exegetical hypotheses can be found as long as we do not simply force our way in at random with a machete. For by doing so we become entangled in a constant struggle with the various theories and, despite every effort, in the end remain entrapped in their contradictions. Instead, what is needed first of all is a kind of aerial photograph of the whole: when our gaze ranges over a larger expanse of terrain, it is also possible to find our bearings. Hence, we must follow the course of exegesis for about a hundred years; it is then that we will spot its major windings and discover what could be called the directional currents along which it has developed. In this way we will learn to discern straight paths from detours. If we attempt such an aerial photographic survey, we can distinguish three generations of exegetes and, corresponding to these, three great principal changes in the history of biblical interpretation in our century. At the beginning of this history stands liberal exegesis, which regards Jesus according to the liberal world picture as the great individualist who liberates religion from cultic institutions and reduces it to ethics, which for its part is founded entirely upon the individual responsibility of conscience. Such a Jesus, who repudiates cultic worship, transforms religion into morality and then defines it as the business of the individual, obviously cannot found a church. He is the foe of all institutions and, therefore, cannot turn around and establish one himself.

The First World War brought with it the collapse of the liberal world and a resulting aversion to its individualism and moralism. The great political bodies, which had relied entirely on science and technology as carriers of the progress of humanity, had failed as forces of ethical order. So the yearning for communion in the sacred was reawakened. There was a rediscovery of the Church, even in the domain of Protestantism. Scandinavian theology witnessed the development of a cultic exegesis, which, in strict antithesis to liberal thought, no longer saw Jesus as a critic of cultic worship but rather understood this worship as the intimate, vital atmosphere of the Bible, in both the Old and the New Testament. Such exegesis, therefore, also attempted to interpret Jesus' words and intentions themselves in the light of the great stream of the lived liturgy. Similar tendencies appeared in the English-speaking world. But even in German Protestantism, a new sense of Church had arisen: there was a growing awareness that the Messiah is unthinkable without his Church.[2] With this renewal of interest in the sacrament, the significance of Jesus' Last Supper as forming communion was now also recognized; the thesis was formulated that Jesus had founded a new community by means of the Last Supper itself and that the Last Supper is the origin of the Church and her permanent rule.[3] Exiled Russian theologians active in France developed the same idea on the basis of the Orthodox tradition into the model of a eucharistic theology that after the Second Vatican Council also came to exercise a powerful influence in Catholicism.[4]

After the Second World War, humanity was divided ever more sharply into two camps: into a world of affluent peoples, who for the most part were once more living according to the liberal model, and into the Marxist block, which conceived of itself both as the spokesman of the poor nations of South America, Africa and Asia

[2] At the end of this movement, F. M. Braun presented a summary of its most significant developments in his still valuable book: *Neues Licht auf die Kirche. Die protestantische Kirchendogmatik in ihrer neuesten Entfaltung* (Einsiedeln, Cologne, 1946 [original French edition: *Aspects nouveaux du problème de l'église*, 1942]).

[3] To my knowledge, this idea was first worked out with full clarity by F. Kattenbusch, "Der Quellort der Kirchenidee", in *Harnack-Festgabe* (1921), 143–72.

[4] Cf., inter alia, P. Evdokimov, *L'Orthodoxie* (Paris, 1959); N. Afanasieff et al., *La Primauté de Pierre dans l'Église orthodoxe* (Neuchâtel, 1960). On the Catholic side: O. Saier, *"Communio" in der Lehre des Zweiten Vatikanischen Konzils* (Munich, 1973); J.-M. Tillard, *Église d'églises: L'Ecclésiologie de communion* (Paris, 1987).

and as their model for the future. Correspondingly, there arose a twofold division of theological tendencies.

In the neoliberal world of the West, a variant of the former liberal theology now became operative in a new guise: the eschatological interpretation of Jesus' message. Jesus, it is true, is no longer conceived as a pure moralist, yet he is once again construed in opposition to the cult and the historical institutions of the Old Testament. This interpretation was a revamping of the old framework that breaks up the Old Testament into priests and prophets: into cult, institution and law, on the one hand, and prophecy, charism and creative freedom, on the other. In this view, priests, cult and institution appear as the negative factor that must be overcome. Jesus, on the other hand, supposedly stands in the prophetic line and fulfills it in antithesis to the priesthood, which is said to have done away with him as it had the prophets.

A new variety of individualism thus comes into being: Jesus now proclaims the end of the institutions. Though his eschatological message may have been conceived according to the mentality of the time as an announcement of the end of the world, it is retrieved for our day as the revolutionary breakthrough from the institutional realm into the charismatic dimension, as the end of the religions, or, in any case, as ''unworldly faith'' that is ceaselessly re-creating its own forms. Once again there can be no question of the foundation of a Church;

such an act would, in fact, contradict this eschatological radicalness.[5]

But this new version of liberalism was quite susceptible to being converted into a Marxist-oriented interpretation of the Bible. The opposition between priests and prophets becomes a cipher for the class struggle, which is taken to be the law of history. Accordingly, Jesus lost his life engaged in combat against the forces of oppression. He is thus transformed into the symbol of the suffering and struggling proletariat, of the "people", as is now more commonly said. The eschatological character of the message then refers to the end of the class-society; the prophet-priest dialectic expresses the dialectic of history, which comes to its final conclusion with the victory of the oppressed and with the emergence of the classless society. The fact that Jesus hardly mentioned the Church, but spoke repeatedly of the Kingdom of God, can be very easily integrated into this view: the "Kingdom" is the classless society, which is held out as the objective toward which the downtrodden people struggles; it is considered as already existing wherever the organized proletariat, that is, its party, socialism, has triumphed.

Ecclesiology now becomes newly significant: it is fitted into the dialectical framework already set up by the division of the Bible into priests and prophets, which is

[5] The work of R. Bultmann established itself as the archetype of this multifariously varied interpretation. Cf., for example, his *Theologie des Neuen Testaments* (Tübingen, 1958).

then conflated with a corresponding distinction between
institution and people. In accordance with this dialectical model, the "popular Church" is pitted against the institutional or "official Church". This "popular Church"
is ceaselessly born out of the people and in this way carries forward Jesus' cause: his struggle against institutions
and their oppressive power for the sake of a new and
free society that will be the "Kingdom".

This is, of course, a very schematic presentation of the
three major phases in the history of the exegesis of the
biblical testimony concerning Jesus and his Church in
the modern period. The variant forms are, taken singly,
endless in number, but the principal line of development
has nonetheless emerged into view.

What does this aerial picture of the exegetical hypotheses of a century show us? Above all it makes evident that the chief exegetical models are borrowed from
the thought pattern of the respective period. Thus, we
get at the truth by extracting from the individual theories their element of contemporary ideology—this is, so
to say, the hermeneutic compass with which our aerial
photograph furnishes us. By the same token, we also
gain new confidence in the internal continuity of the
Church's memory. In both her sacramental life and in
her proclamation of the Word, the Church constitutes a
distinctive subject whose memory preserves the seemingly past word and action of Jesus as a present reality.
This does not imply that the Church has nothing to
learn from the historically evolving currents of theo-

logy. Every new situation of humanity also opens new sides of the human spirit and new points of access to reality. Thus, in her encounter with the historical experiences of humanity, the Church can be led ever more deeply into the truth and perceive new dimensions of it that could not have been understood without these experiences. But skepticism is always in order where new interpretations assail the identity of the Church's memory and replace it with a different mentality, a move that is tantamount to attempting its destruction as memory.

We have thereby gained a second criterion of discernment. We were saying just now that it is necessary to remove from the dominant interpretations of a given epoch that element that originates from contemporary ideology. We can now lay down the converse: compatibility with the base memory of the Church is the standard for judging what is to be considered historically and objectively accurate, as opposed to what does not come from the text of the Bible but has its source in some private way of thinking. Both criteria—the negative criterion of ideology and the positive criterion of the basic ecclesial memory—complement each other and can help us remain as close as possible to the biblical text without disregarding whatever real addition to knowledge the endeavor of the present can have in store for us.

## 2. The witness of the New Testament regarding the origin and essence of the Church

### a. Jesus and the Church

Let us take as our starting point the fact that what Jesus' message immediately announced was not the Church but the kingdom of God (or "the Kingdom of the Heavens"). This can be demonstrated statistically alone by the fact that of the 122 mentions of the Kingdom of God in the New Testament, ninety-nine belong to the synoptic Gospels, of which another ninety uses of the term occur in the sayings of Jesus. One can thus understand the dictum of Loisy, which has since gained popular currency: "Jesus proclaimed the Kingdom; what came was the Church."[6] But a historical reading of the texts reveals that the opposition of Kingdom and Church has no factual basis. For, according to the Jewish interpretation, the gathering and cleansing of men for the King-

[6] E. Peterson, in his famous short treatise of 1929, *Die Kirche* (reprinted in: *Theologische Traktate* [Munich, 1951], 409–29), had been the first to take up this thesis and give it a Catholic twist. I myself probably contributed to its spread by treating it in my lessons and by adopting it from Peterson and Schlier, though in a substantially modified form, in my article "Kirche" in *LThK*. Unfortunately, these alterations have been wiped away in the process of popularization; the maxim was lined with an interpretation that found no support even in Loisy's original meaning. See, for example, L. Boff, *Chiesa, carisma e potere* (Rome, 1983).

dom of God is part of this Kingdom. "Jesus' very belief
that the end was near would have made him desire to
gather the eschatological people of God."[7] In postexilic
prophecy, the coming of the Kingdom is preceded by
the prophet Elijah or by the always anonymous "angel"
who prepares the people for it.

John the Baptist, precisely because he is the herald of
the approaching Messiah, gathers and purifies the community of the end times. In an analogous fashion, Qumran had assembled as a community of the new covenant
precisely because of its eschatological faith. On the basis of this evidence, Jeremias goes so far as to formulate
the following conclusion: "We must reduce the whole
question quite sharply to a single point: the *sole* meaning of the entire activity of Jesus is the gathering of the
eschatological people of God."[8]

Jesus speaks of this people using many images, particularly in the parables having to do with growth. Yet as
he does so, it becomes apparent that the "soon" of the
imminent eschatology characteristic of John the Baptist
and Qumran passes over with Jesus into the "now" of
Christology. Jesus himself is God's action, his coming,
his reigning. In Jesus' mouth, "Kingdom of God" does
not mean some thing or place but the present action
of God. One may therefore translate the programmatic
declaration of Mark 1:15, "the Kingdom of God is near

---

[7] Jeremias, *Neutestamentliche Theologie* (Gütersloh, 1971), 1:167.
[8] Ibid.

at hand", as "God is near." We perceive once more the connection with Jesus, with his person; he himself is God's nearness. Wherever he is, is the Kingdom. In this respect we must recast Loisy's statement: The Kingdom was promised, what came was Jesus. Only in this way can we understand aright the paradox of promise and fulfillment.

But Jesus is never alone. For he came in order to gather together what was dispersed (cf. Jn 11:52; Mt 12:30). His entire work is thus to gather the new people. Hence, this early stage is already marked by the appearance of two elements that are essential for the future understanding of the Church. First, the dynamism of unification, in which men draw together by moving toward God, is a component of the new people of God as Jesus intends it. Second, the point of convergence of this new people is Christ; it becomes a people solely through his call and its response to his call and to his person.

Before we take the next step, I would like to add two more brief remarks to round out what we have said. Among the many images that Jesus utilized for the new people—flock, wedding guests, plantation, God's building, God's city—one stands out as his favorite, that of the family of God. God is the father of the family, Jesus the master of the house, and it therefore stands to reason that he addresses the members of this people as children, even though they are adults, and that to gain true understanding of themselves, those who belong to this people must first lay down their grown-up autonomy and acknowledge themselves as children before God (cf. Mk 10:24; Mt 11:25).[9]

The second observation already leads us to the next topic: the disciples ask Jesus for a special prayer for their community. "Among the religious groups of the surrounding milieu, a special rule of prayer is, in fact, a badge of their community."[10] The request for a prayer thus expresses the disciples' awareness of having become a new community that has its source in Jesus. They appear as the primitive cell of the Church, and they show us at the same time that the Church is a communion united principally on the basis of prayer—of prayer with Jesus, which gives us a shared openness to God.

Two further steps result naturally from this second remark. To begin with, we must take note of the fact that the community of Jesus' disciples is not an amorphous mob. At its center are the Twelve, who form a compactly knit core. This core, according to Luke (10:1–20), is then flanked by the group of the seventy, or, as the case may be, seventy-two. We should bear in mind that the Twelve receive the title "apostles" only after the Resurrection. Previously they had been called simply "the Twelve". This number, which joins them together into a clearly delineated community, is so important that after Judas' betrayal it is once more com-

---

[9] Jeremias, 166.
[10] Ibid.

pleted (Acts 1:15–26). Mark describes their vocation with the phrase "and Jesus made Twelve" (3:14). Their primary task is simply to be the community of the Twelve. Two additional functions then come into play: "that they might be with him and that he might send them" (Mk 3:14).

The symbolic value of the Twelve is consequently of decisive significance: twelve is the number of Jacob's sons, the number of the twelve tribes of Israel. In constituting the circle of Twelve, Jesus presents himself as the patriarch of a new Israel and institutes these twelve men as its origin and foundation. There could be no clearer way of expressing the beginning of a new people, which is now no longer formed by physical descent but by "being with Jesus", a reality that the Twelve receive from him and that he sends them to mediate to others. The theme of unity and plurality may already be descried here as well, although the oneness of the new people is the dominant aspect on account of the inseparable communion of the Twelve, who fulfill their symbolism—their mission—only as twelve.

The group of seventy, or seventy-two, of which Luke speaks supplements this symbolism; seventy (seventy-two) was, according to Jewish tradition (Gen 10; Ex 1:5; Dt 32:8), the number of the non-Jewish peoples of the world.[11] The ascription of the Greek Old Tes-

---

[11] Cf. K. H. Rengstorf, *Das Evangelium nach Lukas* (Göttingen, 1968), 132f.

tament produced in Alexandria to seventy (or seventy-
two) translators was meant to express that, with the
appearance of this Greek text, the sacred book of Israel had become the Bible of all the nations—as subsequently happened in reality thanks to the Christian ap-
propriation of this translation.[12] The seventy disciples
signify the claim of Jesus on the whole of humanity,
which is destined to become the great band of his followers; these seventy are an allusion to the fact that the
new Israel will embrace all the peoples of the earth.

The common prayer that the disciples received from
Jesus leads us onto a further track. During his earthly
life, Jesus had taken part with the Twelve in the temple
worship of Israel. The Our Father was the first stage on
the way toward a special communion of prayer with and
from Jesus. On the night before his Passion, Jesus took
another decisive step beyond this: he transformed the
Passover of Israel into an entirely new worship, which
logically meant a break with the temple community and
thereby definitively established a people of the "New
Covenant". The words of institution of the Eucharist,
whether read in the Markan or in the Pauline tradition,
always have to do with the covenant event; they refer
backward to Sinai and forward to the New Covenant announced by Jeremiah. Moreover, both the Synoptics and

[12] On the significance of the Septuagint, H. Gese, *Vom Sinai zum
Zion*, 2d ed. (Munich, 1984), 16f.; on the evaluation of it in Judaism,
R. Aron, *Die verborgenen Jahre Jesu* (Frankfurt am Mainz., 1962), 209–
17.

John's Gospel, though each in a different way, make the connection with the events of Passover. Finally, there is also an echo of Isaiah's words regarding the suffering servant of God.[13] With Passover and the Sinaiatic covenant ritual, the two founding acts whereby Israel became and ever anew becomes a people are taken up and integrated into the Eucharist. The association of this primordial cultic basis, upon which Israel was founded and by which it lived, with the core words of the prophetic tradition fuses past, present and future in the perspective of a new covenant.

The sense of all this is clear: "Just as the old Israel once revered the temple as its center and the guarantee of its unity, and by its common celebration of the Passover enacted this unity in its own life, in like manner this new meal is now the bond uniting a new people of God. There is no longer any need for a center localized in an outward temple. . . . The Body of the Lord, which is the center of the Lord's Supper, is the one new temple that joins Christians together into a much more real unity than a temple made of stone could ever do."[14]

This is the place to mention yet another series of texts

---

[13] Cf. Jeremias, *Die Abendmahlsworte Jesu* (Göttingen, 1960); J. Betz, *Die Eucharistie in der Zeit der griechischen Väter,* vol. 2, bk. 1: *Die Realpräsenz . . . nach dem Neuen Testament* (Freiburg im Breisgau, 1961); H. Schürmann, *Traditionsgeschichtliche Untersuchungen zu den Evangelien* (Düsseldorf, 1968), 159–247; J. A. Sayes, *El misterio eucarístico* (Madrid, 1986), 3–108.

[14] J. Ratzinger, *Das neue Volk Gottes* (Düsseldorf, 1969), 79.

from the Gospel tradition. Both Matthew and Mark "as well as John hand on (although in diverse contexts) a logion of Jesus according to which in three days he will demolish and rebuild the temple, which he will replace with a better one (Mk 14:58 and Mt 26:61; Mk 15:29 and Mt 27:40; Jn 2:19; cf. Mk 11:15–19 par.; Mt 12:6). It is clear both in the Synoptics and in John that the new temple, 'not made by human hands', is the glorified body of Jesus himself."

This means that "Jesus announces the collapse of the old ritual and, in consequence, of the old people of salvation and the old salvific order and promises a new, higher worship whose center will be his own glorified body."[15]

What conclusion emerges from all the foregoing considerations? The institution of the most holy Eucharist on the evening before the Passion cannot be regarded as some more or less isolated cultic transaction. It is the making of a covenant and, as such, is the concrete foundation of the new people: the people comes into being through its covenant relation to God. We could also say that by his eucharistic action, Jesus draws the disciples into his relationship with God and, therefore, into his mission, which aims to reach "the many", the humanity of all places and of all times. These disciples become a "people" through communion with the Body and Blood of Jesus, which is simultaneously commu-

[15] Ibid., 79f.

nion with God. The Old Testament theme of covenant, which Jesus incorporates into his preaching, receives a new center: communion with Christ's Body. It could be said that the people of the New Covenant takes its origin as a people from the Body and Blood of Christ; solely in terms of this center does it have the status of a people. We can call it "people of God" only because it is through communion with Christ that man gains access to a relationship with God that he cannot establish by his own power.

Looking ahead to our principal theme—the local Church and the universal Church—we can say that the Eucharist, seen as the permanent origin and center of the Church, joins all of the "many", who are now made a people, to the one Lord and to his one and only Body. This fact already implies that the Church and her unity are but one. It is true that the many celebrations in which the one Eucharist will be realized also point ahead to the multiformity of the one Body. Nevertheless, it is clear that these many celebrations cannot stand side by side as autonomous, mutually independent entities but are always simply the presence of one and the same mystery.

### b. The Church's self-description as ἐκκλησία

After this short survey of the acts by which Jesus founded the Church, we still have to turn our attention to the nascent Church of the apostolic period. In this context I would like to stick to two terms whose trail leads to the heart of the apostolic testimony and which follow from the structure we have just discovered in the activity of Jesus: the expression "people of God" and the Pauline idea of the "Body of Christ". By itself, however, the term "people of God" signifies almost without exception the people of Israel and not the Church, for which the vocable ἐκκλησία is used instead; this word subsequently passed over into all the Romance languages and became the proper designation of the new communion that grew out of Jesus' activity.

Why was this word chosen? What is thereby expressed about this communion? Of all the abundant material that modern research has accumulated on this question, I would like to take just one observation. The Greek term that lives on in the Latin loanword *ecclesia* derives from the Old Testament root *qahal*, which is ordinarily translated by "assembly of the people". Such "popular assemblies", in which the people was constituted as a cultic and, on that basis, as a juridical and political entity, existed both in the Greek and the Semitic world.[16]

But there is a twofold distinction between the Old Testament *qahal* and the Greek plenary assembly of en-

---

[16] Cf. L. Rost, *Die Vorstufen von Kirche und Synagoge im Alten Testament. Wortgeschichtliche Untersuchungen* (1938, reprinted 1958); K. L. Schmidt, "καλέω, ἐκκλησία", in: *ThWNT* 3 (1938): 487–539; R. Schnackenburg, *Die Kirche im Neuen Testament*. QD 14 (Freiburg im Breisgau, 1961); H. Schlier, "Ekklesiologie des Neuen Testaments", in: *Mysterium Salutis* 4, 1 (1972), 101–214 (Lit. 215–21).

franchised citizens. Even women and children, who in Greece could not be active agents of political events, belonged to the *qahal*. A closely connected fact is that in Greece it is the males who determine by their decisions what is to be done, while the assembly of Israel gathers "to listen to what God proclaims and to assent to it".[17] This typically biblical conception of the popular assembly is traceable to the fact that the convocation on Sinai was regarded as the normative image of all later such assemblies; it was solemnly reenacted after the Exile by Ezra as the refoundation of the people. But because the dispersion of Israel continued on and slavery was reimposed, a *qahal* coming from God himself, a new gathering and foundation of the people, increasingly became the center of Jewish hope. The supplication for this gathering—for the appearance of the *ecclesia* —is a fixed component of late Jewish prayer.[18]

It is thus clear what it means for the nascent Church to call herself *ecclesia*. By doing so, she says in effect: This petition is granted in us. Christ, who died and rose again, is the living Sinai; those who approach him are the chosen final gathering of God's people (cf., for example, Heb 12:18–24). In this light it becomes comprehensible why the common term "people of God" was not employed to designate the new communion and why the choice fell instead on that expression that stood for

[17] O. Linton, "Ekklesia", in: *RAC* 4:905–21, citation on 907.
[18] Ibid., 907.

the spiritual and eschatological center of the concept of "people". This new communion is first brought into being in the dynamic movement of gathering. Emanating from Christ and sustained by the Holy Spirit, this dynamism has its center in the Lord, who communicates himself in his very Body and Blood. The self-description of the new people as *ecclesia* defines it in terms both of the continuity of the covenant in saving history and of the newness of the mystery of Christ, which is open to what lies ahead. If we must say that "covenant" originally includes "law", righteousness, as an absolutely indispensable component, it follows that now the "new law" becomes the decisive center whose ultimate criterion Christ has established in laying down his life on the Cross.

What has been said also enables us to understand the range of meanings associated with the word *ecclesia* in the New Testament. It signifies not only the cultic gathering but also the local community, the Church in a larger geographical area and, finally, the one Church of Jesus Christ herself. There is a continuous transition from one meaning to another, because all of them hang on the christological center that is made concrete in the gathering of believers for the Lord's Supper. It is always the Lord who in his one sacrifice gathers his one and only people. In all places it is the gathering of this one.

Paul has underlined this aspect with extreme clarity in the Letter to the Galatians. He refers back to the

promise made to Abraham and, using methods typical
of rabbinic exegesis, establishes that in all four texts in
which this promise is communicated to us, it is issued in
the singular—"your seed". Therefore, concludes Paul,
there is only one bearer of the promise, not several. But
how can this be squared with God's universal salvific
will? Through baptism, answers Paul, we are inserted
into Christ and united with him as a single subject;
no longer many alongside one another, but "one only
in Christ Jesus" (Gal 3:16; 26–29). Only Christ's self-
identification with us, only our fusion into unity with
him, makes us bearers of the promise. The ultimate goal
at which this gathering aims is perfect unity—it is "unification" with the Son, which at the same time makes
it possible to enter into the living unity of God himself,
so that God might be all in all (1 Cor 15:28).

### c. The Pauline doctrine of
### the Church as the Body of Christ

It follows, then, that it is entirely impossible to conceive of the New Testament's notion of the people of
God apart from Christology, which in turn is no ab-
stract theory but a concrete event taking place in the
sacraments of baptism and the Eucharist. In these sacraments, Christology opens up into the Trinity. For it is
the risen Christ alone who can be this infinite breadth
and openness; but of him Saint Paul says "the Lord is
the Spirit" (2 Cor 3:17). In the Spirit we say together

with Christ "Abba", because we have become sons (cf. Rom 8:15; Gal 4:6). Paul has thus by no means created anything new when he calls the Church the "Body of Christ"; he simply offers a short formula for the reality that from the very beginning shaped the development of the Church.

The oft-repeated assertion that Paul merely applied to the Church an allegory widely current in the Stoic philosophy of his time is totally false.[19] The Stoic allegory compares the state to an organism whose members must all work together. This metaphor is an image for the reciprocal dependence of all on all and, therefore, also for the importance of the diverse functions that build up a commonwealth. This imaginative picture was used in order to calm agitated masses and to recall them to their specific tasks; every organ has a significance proper to it alone; it is absurd for all to want to be the same organ, because the result is not the elevation of all but rather the reciprocal abasement and destruction of all.

It is indisputable that Paul also had recourse to such notions, as, for example, when he tells the quarreling Corinthians that it would indeed be ridiculous for the foot to want suddenly to be a hand, or for the ear to conceive a sudden desire to be an eye: "If the whole body becomes an eye, what about the hearing? And if everything becomes an ear, what about the sense of smell? But

[19] See on this point the thorough article "σῶμα", by E. Schweizer, in: *ThWNT* 7:1024–91.

God has set each one of the members as he willed. . . .
There are many members, but the body is one" (1 Cor
12:17ff.). However, Saint Paul's conception of the Body
of Christ does not exhaust itself in considerations of so-
ciology or moral philosophy such as these; if this were
so, it would be nothing but a marginal gloss on the actual substantive content of the notion of the Church.
Even in the pre-Christian world of Greece and Rome,
the image of the body had a broader range of meaning.
The Platonic idea that the entire world is *one* body, one
living being, was developed in Stoic philosophy, where
it was associated with the belief that the world was divine. But it is not our intention to treat of this matter
here. For the real roots of the Pauline idea of the Body
of Christ are entirely inner-biblical. Three sources of
this idea can be identified in the biblical tradition.

In the first place, the Semitic conception of the "corporate personality" stands in the background; this conception is expressed, for example, in the idea that we
are all Adam, a single man writ large. In the modern
era, with its apotheosis of the subject, this notion became entirely incomprehensible. The "I" was now a
fortified stronghold with impassable walls. Descartes'
attempt to derive the whole of philosophy from the
"*cogito*"—because only the "I" still appeared accessible in any way—is typical in this regard. Today the
concept of subject is gradually unraveling; it is becoming evident that the "I" locked securely in itself does
not exist but that various influences pass in and out of

us.[20] At the same time there is a renewed understanding that the "I" is constituted in relation to the "thou" and that the two mutually interpenetrate. Thus, the Semitic view of the corporate personality—without which it is difficult to enter into the notion of the Body of Christ—could once again become more easily accessible.

But the Pauline formula has in addition two more concrete roots. The first lies in the Eucharist, by which the Lord himself virtually invited this conception. "The bread we break, is it not participation in the body of Christ? Because it is one bread, we, the many, are one body", says Paul to the Corinthians, that is, in the same letter in which he first develops the doctrine of the Body of Christ (1 Cor 10:16f.). It is here that we find the true basis of this doctrine: the Lord becomes our bread, our food. He gives us his body, which, by the way, must be understood in the light of the Resurrection and of the Semitic linguistic background of Saint Paul. The body is a man's self, which does not coincide with the corporeal dimension but comprises it as one element among others. Christ gives us himself—Christ, who in his Resurrection has continued to exist in a new kind of bodili-

---

[20] See J. Baur, *Einsicht und Glaube* (Göttingen, 1978), 43f. This unraveling of subjectivity is a theme strongly emphasized in the work of the Tübingen philosopher W. Schulz (*Ich und Welt*, 1979; *Metaphysik des Schwebens*, 1985; *Grundprobleme der Ethik*, 1989); brief information about Schulz' work can be found in T. J. Wetz, *Tübinger Triade: Zum Werk von W. Schulz* (Pfullingen, 1990).

ness. The outward action of eating becomes the expression of that intimate penetration of two subjects that we examined briefly just now. Communion means that the seemingly uncrossable frontier of my "I" is left wide open and can be so because Jesus has first allowed himself to be opened completely, has taken us all into himself and has put himself totally into our hands. Hence, Communion means the fusion of existences; just as in the taking of nourishment the body assimilates foreign matter to itself, and is thereby enabled to live, in the same way my "I" is "assimilated" to that of Jesus, it is made similar to him in an exchange that increasingly breaks through the lines of division. This same event takes place in the case of all who communicate; they are all assimilated to this "bread" and thus are made one among themselves—*one* body.

In this way Communion makes the Church by breaching an opening in the walls of subjectivity and gathering us into a deep communion of existence. It is the event of "gathering", in which the Lord joins us to one another. The formula "the Church is the Body of Christ" thus states that the Eucharist, in which the Lord gives us his body and makes us one body, forever remains the place where the Church is generated, where the Lord himself never ceases to found her anew; in the Eucharist the Church is most compactly herself—in all places, yet one only, just as he is one only.

These reflections bring us to the third root of Paul's notion of the Body of Christ: the idea of nuptiality, or

—to express it in profane terms—the biblical philosophy of love, which is inseparable from eucharistic theology. This philosophy of love appears immediately at the beginning of Holy Scripture: it is found at the conclusion of the creation narrative, where the following prophetic word is attributed to Adam: "For this reason the man shall leave his father and mother and cleave to the woman, and they shall become *one* flesh" (Gen 2:24). *One* flesh—hence, a single new existence. Paul also takes up this idea that man and woman become one flesh in a bond at once spiritual and physical in the First Letter to the Corinthians, where he states that this word is fulfilled in communion: "He who cleaves to the Lord becomes one spirit with him" (1 Cor 6:17). Once again we must not interpret the term "spirit" with modern linguistic sensibilities but must read it in its Pauline sense; if we do so, its significance is not far removed from "body". It means a single spiritual existence together with him who, in rising again, was made "spirit" by the Holy Spirit while remaining bodily in the openness of this Spirit.

What we developed previously in terms of the image of eating now becomes more perspicuous and more comprehensible from the point of view of the image of love between human beings: in the sacrament, which is an act of love, two subjects are fused in such a way as to overcome their separation and to be made one. Hence, the eucharistic mystery, precisely in being transformed by the idea of nuptiality, remains the heart of the concept of the Church as described by the term "Body of Christ".

But a new, more important aspect, which might be ignored in a narrowly conceived sacramental theology, now emerges: the Church is the Body of Christ in the way in which the woman is one body, or rather one flesh, with the man. Put in other terms, the Church is the Body, not by virtue of an identity without distinction, but rather by means of the pneumatic-real act of spousal love. Expressed in yet another way, this means that Christ and the Church are one body in the sense in which man and woman are one flesh, that is, in such a way that in their indissoluble spiritual-bodily union, they nonetheless remain unconfused and unmingled. The Church does not simply become Christ, she is ever the handmaid whom he lovingly raises to be his Bride and who seeks his face throughout these latter days.

Yet against the backdrop of the indicative intimated in the words "Bride" and "Body", the imperative of Christian existence also emerges, making plain the dynamic character of sacramental reality, which is not an already accomplished physical fact but takes place as a personal event. It is precisely the mystery of love, seen as a nuptial mystery, that indicates in unmistakable terms both our task and the Church's capacity to fall short of it. The Church must constantly become what she is through unitive love and resist the temptation to fall from her vocation into the infidelity of self-willed autonomy. The relational and pneumatological character of the notions of the Body of Christ and of nuptiality becomes evident, as does the reason why the Church is never complete but is perpetually in need of renewal. She is always on the way to union with Christ, which also includes the Church's own internal unity. By the same token, the Church's unity becomes all the more fragile, the farther she distances herself from this fundamental relationship.

### 3. The vision of the Church in the Acts of the Apostles

In the course of these reflections we have considered only a small, though—in my opinion—important portion of the New Testament's witness concerning the origin and essence of the Church; only if we have in mind these few main points can we find the right answers to the questions that agitate us today in every quarter. The criterion governing my selection was that it is indispensable at the outset to ascertain as far as possible what Jesus himself intended for the Church.

I have tried to disengage the core of the postpaschal testimony concerning the Church by investigating the name with which the new communion originating from Jesus preferred to call itself: *ecclesia*. The choice of this name expressed a theological option that answers to the fundamental intentions of Jesus' preaching. To complete the picture, it would be useful to pursue now yet other strands of the New Testament tradition. An analysis of the Acts of the Apostles, which in its totality could be described as a narrative ecclesiology, would be particularly fruitful.[21] On the other hand, this would far exceed the limits set us here. Thus, without entering into details, I would like merely to point out by way of conclusion that at the very beginning of this fundamentally important book about the origin and essence of the Church, Luke portrays this essence using three images, which express more than can be captured in concepts.

The first image is that of the disciples' retreat in the cenacle: here the apostles and the entire small community of believers in Jesus are gathered with Mary and persevere unanimously in prayer. In this scene every detail is important: the cenacle, the "upper room", as the context in which the Church is born; the Eleven, who are listed by name; Mary, the women and the brethren —it is a genuine *qahal*, a covenant assembly with diverse orders, which is at the same time a mirror of the entire new people. This convocation abides with

---

[21] I have attempted to set forth a few elements of the testimony of the Acts of the Apostles in my book *Behold the Pierced One* (San Francisco, 1986), 71ff. For the rest, see the commentaries, esp. G. Schneider, *Die Apostelgeschichte*, vol. 1 (Freiburg im Breisgau, 1980) and vol. 2 (1982); R. Pesch, "Die Apostelgeschichte", in *EKK* 1 and 2 (Zurich, 1986).

one mind in prayer and thus receives its unity from
the Lord. Its action is essentially to turn to the living
God—to become open to his will. The number 120
contains a clear allusion to the number twelve, to its
sacral character rooted in the promise, as well as to its
future destiny of worldwide growth and development.
Finally, Peter appears as one who speaks and acts, thus
exercising the responsibility committed to him by the
Lord to strengthen his brethren (Lk 22:32).

The completion of the circle of the Twelve by the
election of Matthias reveals the interplay of personal action and obedience to God, who is the primary agent:
the decision by lot makes it apparent that all action
on the part of the assembled community is strictly
preparatory. The final decision in the proper sense is
left to God's will. Here too the community remains
"in prayer": it is not transformed into a parliament, but
shows what *qahal*, what Church, is.

The second image is found at the end of the second chapter, where the primitive Church, which at this
point has already come into being, is depicted in terms
of a fourfold adherence: adherence to the teaching of
the apostles, which is already a preview of the apostolic succession and of the official witness entrusted
to the successors of the apostles, to the community,
to the breaking of the bread and to the prayers. One
could say that word and sacrament appear here as the
two mainstays of the living edifice of the Church. But
it is necessary to add that this word is tied to the in-

stitutional role and personal responsibility of the witness. We must further add that the designation of the
sacrament as the "breaking of bread" expresses the so-
cial requirement of the Eucharist, which is not an isolated cultic act but a way of existence: life in sharing, in
communion with Christ, who gives the gift of his very
self.

Between these two images stands Saint Luke's depic-
tion of Pentecost: vehement wind and fire of the Holy
Ghost establish the Church. The origin of the Church
is not the decision of men; she is not the product of
human willing but a creature of the Spirit of God. This
Spirit overcomes the Babylonian world spirit. Man's
will to power, symbolized in Babel, aims at the goal
of uniformity, because its interest is domination and
subjection; it is precisely in this way that it brings forth
hatred and division. God's Spirit, on the other hand,
is love; for this reason he brings about recognition and
creates unity in the acceptance of the otherness of the
other: the many languages are mutually comprehensible.

There are two aspects of this scene that we must un-
derscore on account of their importance for our overall
theme. The image of Pentecost presented in the Acts of
the Apostles shows the interplay of plurality and unity
and in this sense teaches us to perceive the distinctive
character of the Holy Spirit as opposed to the spirit of
the world. The spirit of the world subjugates, the Holy
Spirit opens. The Church embraces the many languages,

that is, the many cultures, that in faith understand and fecundate one another. In this respect it can be said that we find here a preliminary sketch of a Church that lives in manifold and multiform particular Churches but that precisely in this way is the one Church. At the same time, Luke expresses with this image the fact that at the moment of her birth, the Church was already catholic, already a world Church. Luke thus rules out a conception in which a local Church first arose in Jerusalem and then became the base for the gradual establishment of other local Churches that eventually grew into a federation. Luke tells us that the reverse is true: what first exists is the one Church, the Church that speaks in all tongues—the *ecclesia universalis*; she then generates Church in the most diverse locales, which nonetheless are all always embodiments of the one and only Church. The temporal and ontological priority lies with the universal Church; a Church that was not catholic would not even have ecclesial reality. . . .

In his Pentecost account, Luke has very subtly woven the historical dynamism of this catholicity into the narrative and, in so doing, has also anticipated the arc of tension of his entire story. In order to express the catholicity of the Church created by the Holy Spirit, he has made use of an old, presumably Hellenistic, scheme of twelve peoples. This scheme is closely related to the lists of nations compiled in the states that succeeded the empire of Alexander. Luke enumerates these twelve peoples and their languages as receivers of the apostolic word, yet at the end he breaks out of the scheme by adding a thirteenth people: the Romans.[22]

But the whole Book of Acts is arranged, not according to purely historiographical concerns, but on the basis of a theological idea. It portrays the path of the Gospel from the Jews to the Gentiles and thus depicts the fulfillment of the commission with which Jesus left his disciples: to be his witnesses "to the ends of the earth" (Acts 1:8). However, in the general plan of the book, the path of the witnesses—in particular of Saint Paul—from Jerusalem to Rome becomes in turn a graphic synthesis of this theological way. In Luke's presentation, Rome is the recapitulation of the pagan world as such. "Paul's arrival in Rome marks the goal of the path that began in Jerusalem; the universal—the catholic—Church has been realized, in continuance of the ancient chosen people and its history and taking over the latter's mission. Thus Rome, as a symbol for the world of the nations, has a theological status in Acts; it cannot be separated from the Lukan idea of catholicity."[23]

One may therefore say that Luke anticipates all the chief questions of the postapostolic period and with his interplay of multiplicity and unity, universality and particularity, gives us a guide that helps us understand our problems in the light of the testimony of the origin.

---

[22] Cf. G. Schneider, 253ff.; R. Pesch, 105f.
[23] Ratzinger, *Behold the Pierced One*, 73.

# II

# The Primacy of Peter and the Unity of the Church

The question of the primacy of Peter and of its continuation in the bishops of Rome is probably the most difficult problem of the ecumenical dispute. Even in the Catholic Church herself, the Roman primacy has again and again proved to be a stumbling block, from the medieval struggle between *imperium* and *sacerdotium*, through the early modern state Church movements and the nineteenth century's demands for independence from Rome, up to the contemporary surges of protest against the pope's function of leadership and his mode of exercising it. Nevertheless, there is also a positive tendency today. Many non-Catholics affirm the necessity of a common center of Christianity. It is becoming evident that only such a center can be an effective protection against the drift into dependence on political systems or the pressures emanating from our civilization; that only by having such a center can the faith of Christians secure a clear voice in the confusion of ideologies. All of this forces us in our treatment of the subject to lend an especially attentive ear to the witness of the Bible and to inquire with particular care into the faith of the nascent Church.

More precisely, we must distinguish two principal problems. The first may be defined in the following terms: Was there ever such a thing as the primacy at all? Since this can be denied only with difficulty in the face of the New Testament evidence, we must formulate the question more precisely. What is the actual meaning of the preeminence of Peter, to which the New Testament attests in so many ways?

Even more complex and in many regards more decisive is the second question we must take up: Can a Petrine succession really be justified on the basis of the New Testament? Does the New Testament call for it, or does it rule it out? And if the succession is admitted, can Rome lay a legitimate claim to being its seat?

Let us begin with the first complex of problems.

## 1. The status of Peter in the New Testament

It would be misguided to pounce immediately on the classic proof text for the primacy, Matthew 16:13–20. The isolation of an individual text always renders comprehension more difficult. Instead of proceeding in this way, let us approach the subject in concentric circles. Let us, then, first investigate the image of Peter in the New Testament as a whole and then elucidate the figure of Peter in the Gospels. This will enable us to reach an understanding of the specific texts concerning the primacy.

### a. The mission of Peter in the whole of
### New Testament tradition

It is immediately striking that all the major groups of texts in the New Testament are acquainted with the subject of Peter, which is thereby proven to be a topic of universal significance whose importance cannot be restricted to a particular tradition limited to one person or place.[1] In the Pauline corpus we come upon a first weighty piece of evidence in the ancient formula of faith transmitted by the apostle in 1 Corinthians 15:3–7. Cephas—note how Paul names the apostle from Bethsaida using the Aramaic word for rock—is introduced as the first witness of the Resurrection of Jesus Christ. In this connection we must bear in mind that it is none other than Paul who views the essence of apostleship as witness to the Resurrection of Christ: indeed, according to his own testimony, Paul is entitled to consider himself an apostle in the full sense because the risen Lord appeared to him and called him.

We thus begin to grasp something of the weight of the fact that Peter had the privilege of being the first to see the Lord and that he entered into the confession formulated by the primitive community as the first witness. We may even see in this circumstance something like a new installation in the primacy, in the first rank

[1] On the image of Peter in the individual writings of the New Testament, see R. Pesch, *Simon-Petrus* (Stuttgart, 1980), 135–52.

among the apostles. When we add to this that we are dealing with a very ancient pre-Pauline formula, which Paul transmits with great reverence as an unassailably secure part of the tradition, the significance of the text is plain for all to see.

It is true that the polemical Letter to the Galatians also shows us a Paul who is in conflict with Peter and who defends his own independent vocation to be an apostle. It is precisely this polemical context that gives the Letter's witness to Peter all the greater significance. Paul goes up to Jerusalem to "meet Peter"—"*videre Petrum*" is the Vulgate's translation (Gal 1:18). "I did not see any of the other apostles", he adds, "except James, the brother of the Lord." But the aim of the visit is limited precisely to encountering Peter.

Fourteen years later, Paul, in obedience to a revelation, makes his way once more to the holy city, where he now calls upon the three pillars, James, Cephas and John, this time with a very clearly defined purpose. He submits to them his gospel, just as he preaches it among the Gentiles, "so that I might not run in vain or have run in vain"—a statement of great import, considering the self-assurance of the apostle to the Gentiles and the general tenor of the letter: there is only *one* common gospel, and the certainty that one is announcing the right message is tied to communion with the three pillars. They are the criterion. The contemporary reader feels himself compelled to ask how this triumvirate was formed and what Peter's position in it was. As a matter of fact, O. Cullmann has propounded the thesis that Peter must have had to cede the primacy to James some time after the year 42; he is not alone in thinking that John's Gospel reflects rivalry between John and Peter.[2]

It would be interesting to investigate these questions, but such an inquiry would take us too far afield from the present subject. To all appearances James exercised a sort of primacy over Jewish Christianity, whose center was Jerusalem. However, this primacy never attained a significant role in the universal Church, and it disappeared from history with the downfall of Jewish Christianity. The special rank of John was of another sort, as can be seen quite well from the Fourth Gospel. Thus, one may suppose without controversy a kind of primacy of three during the phase of the Church's organizational development described in the Letter to the Galatians. Nonetheless, the priority of each of the three has diverse reasons and is of a different nature. In consequence, however one defines in detail the way in which the pillars coexisted within the group of three, the unique primacy of Peter, which goes back to the Lord himself, remains unaffected by the common function of being "a pillar",

[2] O. Cullmann, *Petrus-Jünger-Apostel-Märtyrer* (Zurich, 1952), 253 and 259; Martin Hengel has recently reexamined this question in a detailed and thorough study, "Jakobus der Herrenbruder—der erste Papst?", in: *Glaube und Eschatologie. Festschrift für W. Kümmel* (Tübingen, 1985), 71–104. On Paul's portrait of Peter, see especially F. Mußner, *Petrus und Paulus: Pole der Einheit*. QD 76 (Freiburg, 1976), 77–89.

and the fact stands that every proclamation of the gospel must gauge itself by the preaching of Peter. In addition, the Letter to the Galatians attests that this primacy is also valid when the first apostle falls short of his mission in his personal conduct (Gal 2:11–14).

If, after this cursory glance at the testimony of Paul, we pass to the Johannine writings, we find that Peter is markedly present as a counterpoint to the figure of the beloved disciple; this tendency persists through the whole Gospel and reaches its culmination in the great mission pericope, John 21:15–19. No one less than R. Bultmann has stated plainly that in this text Peter is "entrusted with the supreme leadership of the Church";[3] he even sees in it the original version of the tradition recurring in Matthew 16 and considers the passage to be an ancient fragment of pre-Johannine tradition. His thesis, that Peter's authority nonetheless interested the evangelist only so that he might claim it for the beloved disciple after it had been, so to speak, orphaned by the death of Peter, finds no support either in the text or in the history of the Church. On the other hand, Bultmann's hypothesis does show that it is impossible to dodge the question of what Jesus' words about Peter mean after the latter's death. What is important here for us is that alongside Paul, the Johannine strand of tradition also offers quite unmistakable evidence for the

[3] R. Bultmann, *Das Evangelium des Johannes*, 15th ed. (Göttingen, 1957), 552, n. 3.

awareness that Peter enjoyed a position of primacy that came to him from the Lord.

Finally, we find in each one of the synoptic Gospels independent traditions regarding the same subject, so that it once again becomes plain to what degree this motif belongs to the basic form of Christian proclamation and is present in all the streams of New Testament tradition: among the Jewish Christians, in Antioch, in Paul's missionary territory and in Rome. For the sake of brevity we must dispense with the analysis of all the important individual texts and must even forego a consideration of Luke's version of the primacy commission, "strengthen your brethren" (Lk 22:32), which anchors Peter's mission in the event of the Last Supper, thus giving it a significant ecclesiological emphasis. Instead of this, I would like to indicate in a more general way the special position that all three of the synoptic Gospels, even prescinding from Matthew 16, accord to Peter.

### b. Peter in the group of the Twelve according to the synoptic tradition

In this matter we can begin with the observation that in general Peter enjoys a special position in the circle of the Twelve. Together with the sons of Zebedee, he constitutes a group of three that stands out prominently among the twelve apostles. They alone are admitted to two moments of particular consequence—the Transfiguration and the Garden of Olives (Mk 9:2ff.; 14:33ff.); likewise

only these three are permitted to witness the raising of
Jairus' young daughter (Mk 5:37). In turn, Peter is preeminent among the three; he is the spokesman in the
Transfiguration scene; it is he whom the Lord addresses
in his hour of anguish in the Garden of Olives. In Luke
5:1–11, the calling of Peter appears as the original pattern of apostolic vocation par excellence. Peter is also
the one who attempts to walk upon the sea in imita-
tion of the Lord (Mt 14:28ff.); after the conferral of
the power to bind and loose, he asks how often one
ought to pardon (Mt 18:21). All of this is underlined
by Peter's ranking in the lists of the disciples. These lists
are known to us in four versions (Mt 10:2–4; Mk 3:16–
19; Lk 6:14–16; Acts 1:13), which vary in many points
of detail but which all unanimously name Peter at the
head. In Matthew's Gospel, he is even introduced with
the momentous word "the first"—the root that in the
later language of "primacy" became the term for the
special mission of the fisherman from Bethsaida makes
itself heard here for the first time. The substance of the
same fact is expressed when in Mark 1:36 and Luke 9:32
the disciples are introduced with the formula "Peter and
those with him".

This point leads us to a second important element:
the new name that Jesus bestowed on the apostle. It is
—as the Protestant exegete Schulze-Kadelbach has ob-
served—one of "the things that we know with most
certainty about this man": that he was called by the title "rock" and that this was not his original name but

rather the new name that Jesus gave him.[4] Paul—as we have seen—still makes use of the Aramaic form that comes from the mouth of Jesus and names the apostle "Kephas". The fact that this word was translated and the apostle thus went down in history with the Greek title of "Peter" confirms beyond question that this was no proper name,[5] for proper names are not translated. Now it was not at all uncommon for rabbis to bestow surnames on their disciples; Jesus himself gave this sort of name to the sons of Zebedee, whom he called "Sons of Thunder" (Mk 3:17). But how are we to understand the new first name Peter? It certainly does not portray the character of this man whom Flavius Josephus' description of the Galilean national temperament so recognizably fits: "brave, kind-hearted, trusting, but also easily influenced and eager for change".[6] The designation "rock" yields no pedagogical or psychological meaning; it can be understood only in terms of mystery, that is to say, christologically and ecclesiologically: Simon Peter will be by Jesus' commission precisely what he is not by "flesh and blood". J. Jeremias has shown that in the background stands the symbolic language of the holy rock. A rabbinical text may shed some light on what is meant here: "Yahweh spoke: 'How can I create the

---

[4] G. Schulze-Kadelbach, "Die Stellung des Petrus in der Urchristenheit", in: *Theol. Lit.-Ztg.* 81: (1956) 1–14; citation on 4.

[5] O. Cullmann, "Πέτρος, Κῆφας", in: *ThWNT* 6:99–112; citation, 100.

[6] Cited by Schulze-Kadelbach, 4.

world, when these godless men will arise to vex me?'
But when God looked upon Abraham, who was also to
be born, he spoke: 'Behold, I have found a rock upon
which I can build and found the world.' He therefore
called Abraham a rock: 'Look upon the rock from which
you have been hewn' (Is 51:12)."[7] Abraham, the father
of faith, is by his faith the rock that holds back chaos,
the onrushing primordial flood of destruction, and thus
sustains creation. Simon, the first to confess Jesus as the
Christ and the first witness of the Resurrection, now
becomes by virtue of his Abrahamic faith, which is renewed in Christ, the rock that stands against the impure
tide of unbelief and its destruction of man.

We may thus say that in reality the very act of naming
the fisherman from Bethsaida the "rock"—which is a
wholly incontrovertible fact—already contains the entire theology of Matthew 16:18 and is therefore a guarantee of its authenticity.

### c. The commission logion: Matthew 16:17-19

We must now examine this central text of the Petrine
tradition somewhat more closely. Considering the significance that this utterance of the Lord about binding
and loosing has been accorded in the Catholic Church,
it comes as no surprise that all the vicissitudes of confes-
sional polemics are reflected in the interpretation of it, as

[7] J. Jeremias, *Golgotha und der heilige Fels* (Leipzig, 1926), 74.

are also the variations within Catholic theology itself.[8] Whereas liberal Protestant theology had found reasons to contest the origin of these words from Jesus, between the Wars there emerged even among Protestant theologians a sort of consensus that almost uniformly accepted their provenance from the Lord. In the new theological climate that arose after the Second World War, this consensus rather rapidly crumbled away again. It is not at all astonishing that in the atmosphere of the postconciliar period, even Catholic exegetes dissociated themselves more and more from the position that this logion has its origin in Jesus.[9] There is now a search for situations in the early Church into which the saying is supposed to fit, and the exegetes think predominantly—seconding Bultmann—of the oldest Palestinian community, or of Jerusalem, or else of Antioch, where they attempt to locate the composition of Matthew's Gospel. Of course there are still other voices; for example, J. M. van Cangh and M. van Esbroeck, drawing on observations of H. Riesenfeld, have once more brought to light the Jewish context of Matthew's account and, in the process, have published noteworthy findings that both confirm the great antiquity of the text and make evident that

---

[8] A short overview of the problem in the history of exegesis can be found in Cullmann, *Petrus*, 176–90.

[9] See, for example, A. Sand, *Das Evangelium nach Matthäus* (Regensburg, 1986), 333 ("Wort des Auferweckten", "Wort in die nachösterliche Gemeinde"); J. Gnilka moves cautiously in the same direction, in: *Das Matthäusevangelium* (Freiburg im Breisgau, 1988), 2:77.

it possesses an even greater theological depth than was
hitherto recognized.[10]

We cannot enter into all these debates here; nor is it
necessary for us to do so. There are two reasons why
this is the case. First, we have seen that the substance
of what Matthew says is mirrored in all the strata of
New Testament tradition, however diversely these lay-
ers may be organized in other respects. Such unity of
the tradition can be explained only if what is recounted
in Matthew originates from Jesus himself. Second, we
have no need to pursue these discussions further in a
theological reflection, because for one who in the faith
of the Church reads the Bible as the Word of God, the
validity of a given statement does not depend upon the
historical hypotheses concerning its most ancient form
and source. Everyone who attends to the findings of the
exegetes over a longer period of time knows how short-
lived these hypotheses are. A saying of Jesus reported in
the Bible is not made binding on faith because it is acknowledged as Jesus' word by the majority of contemporary exegetes, and it does not lose its validity when
the opposite is the case. It is valid because Holy Scripture is valid and because Scripture presents it to us as an
utterance of Jesus. Said in other terms: the guarantee of
its validity does not result from hypothetical constructs,
however well founded they might be, but from inclu-

[10] J. M. van Cangh-M. van Esbroeck, "La Primauté de Pierre (Mt
16, 16–19) et son contexte judaique", in: *Rev. théol. de Louvain* 11
(1980): 310–24.

sion in the canon of Scripture, which in turn the faith of the Church avouches as the Word of God, that is, as the trustworthy ground of our existence.

Once we accept this condition, it is, of course, important to understand as precisely as possible the structure and contents of a text using the methods of historical reasoning. In essence, the principal objection of the liberal epoch against the origin of the vocation logion from Jesus himself was the observation that it employs the term "Church" (ἐκκλησία), whose occurrence in the Gospels is limited exclusively to this passage and to Matthew 18:17. Since—as was shown in the first chapter—it was taken for granted that Jesus could not have intended a church, this linguistic usage appeared to be a telltale anachronism, which had to be indicative of the late creation of the word in the already existing Church. On the other hand, the Protestant exegete A. Oepke has drawn attention to the fact that one cannot be cautious enough with such verbal statistics. He points out, for example, that the word "cross" does not occur in the whole of Saint Paul's Letter to the Romans, although the letter is imbued from beginning to end with the apostle's theology of the Cross.[11]

Hence, compared with word frequencies, the literary form of the text is of much greater weight. Concerning Matthew 16:17–19, even the undisputed leader of liberal

[11] A. Oepke, *Der Herrenspruch über die Kirche Mt 16, 17–19 in der neuesten Forschung*, Studia Theologica (Lund, 1948–1950), 114; cf. Cullmann, *Petrus*, 209.

theology himself—A. von Harnack—has said: "There
are not many longer sections in the Gospels from which
the Aramaic basis shines through in form and content
so surely as from this tightly compact pericope."[12] Bultmann formulates a very similar statement: "I cannot see
that the conditions for its composition would have existed anywhere other than in the primitive community
at Jerusalem."[13] The introductory phrase "blessed are
you" is Aramaic, as is the unexplained name Barjona,
and, furthermore, the terms "gates of the underworld",
"keys of the kingdom of heaven", "bind and loose", "on
earth and in heaven". The play on the word "rock" (you
are rock and upon this rock . . .) does not work with
complete success in Greek, where it is now necessary
to switch gender from Petros to Petra: we can thus hear
even through this pun the Aramaic word *kepha* and perceive the voice of Jesus himself.[14]

Let us proceed to the exegesis, which again can deal
only with a few chief points. We have already spoken
about the symbolism of the rock and have seen that Peter
is cast in a role parallel to Abraham's; his function for
the new people, the *ecclesia*, has—as befits the status of

[12] Quoted from J. R. Geiselmann, *Der petrinische Primat* (Münster,
1927), 9.

[13] Ibid. Cf. *Theologie des Neuen Testaments*, 3d ed. (Tübingen, 1958),
51.

[14] The more recent attempt of C. C. Caragounis, *Peter and the Rock*
(Berlin, New York, 1990), to refer the word rock, not to Simon
Peter, but to his confession of faith is just as unconvincing as ear-
lier interpretations of this sort.

this people—cosmic and eschatological significance. In order to understand the way in which Peter is a rock, a quality he does not have of himself, it is useful to keep in mind how Matthew continues the narrative. It was not by "flesh and blood" but by the revelation of the Father that he had confessed Christ in the name of the Twelve. When Jesus subsequently explains the figure and the destiny of the Christ in this world, prophesying death and resurrection, it is flesh and blood that respond: Peter "scolds the Lord": "By no means shall this ever be" (16:22). To which Jesus replies: "Be gone, behind me, Satan; you are a stumbling block (*skandalon*) for me" (16:23). Left to his own resources, the one who by God's grace is permitted to be the bedrock is a stone on the path that makes the foot stumble.

The tension between the gift coming from the Lord and man's own capacity is rousingly portrayed in this scene, which in some sense anticipates the entire drama of papal history. In this history we repeatedly encounter two situations. On the one hand, the papacy remains the foundation of the Church in virtue of a power that does not derive from herself. At the same time, individual popes have again and again become a scandal because of what they themselves are as men, because they want to precede, not follow, Christ, because they believe that they must determine by their own logic the path that only Christ himself can decide: "You do not think God's thoughts, but man's" (Mt 16:23).

We find a parallel to the promise that the power of

death will not be able to prevail against the rock (or the Church?) in the vocation of the prophet Jeremiah, to whom it is said at the beginning of his mission: "And behold—I am making you today a fortified city, a pillar of iron, a wall of bronze against the whole land, against the kings of Judah, its officials, its priests and the people of the land. They will fight against you and yet not vanquish you, for I am with you to rescue you" (1:18f.).

What A. Weiser writes a propos of this word of the Old Testament can also serve perfectly well as an exegesis of the promise of Jesus concerning Peter: "God demands the entire courage of an unreserved trust in his prodigious power when he promises the seemingly impossible: that he will make this soft man into a 'fortified city', an 'iron pillar' and a 'bronze wall', that Jeremiah will stand alone like a living wall of God against the whole land and those who wield power in it. . . . It is not the inviolability of the 'consecrated' man of God that will protect him against harm . . . but only the proximity of God, who 'rescues' him, so that his foes will not be able to prevail against him (cf. Mt 16:18)."[15] However, the promise to Peter is more sweeping than that which was given to the prophet of the Old Testament. Whereas mere powers of flesh and blood were pitted against the prophet, the gates of hell, the destructive powers of the abyss, are ranged against Peter. Jeremiah receives only a personal promise for his service as a prophet; Peter

[15] A. Weiser, *Das Buch Jeremia*, 5th ed. (Göttingen, 1966), 11.

receives a promise for the time-transcendent gathering of the new people—a gathering that stretches beyond his own lifetime. This is why Harnack believed that the Lord's promise is a prophecy of Peter's immortality, and in a certain sense this is correct: the rock will not be overcome, because God does not abandon his *ecclesia* to the powers of destruction.

The power of the keys recalls the word of God to Eliakim recorded in Isaiah 22:22. Along with the keys, Eliakim receives in trust "dominion and control over the dynasty of the descendants of David".[16] But the word that the Lord addresses to the doctors of the law and the Pharisees, whom he reproaches for shutting the doors of the Kingdom of Heaven to men (Mt 23:13), also helps us to comprehend the content of this commission logion. As the faithful steward of Jesus' message, Peter opens the door to the Kingdom of Heaven; his is the function of doorkeeper, who has to judge concerning admission and rejection (cf. Rev 3:7). In this sense, the significance of the reference to the keys clearly approximates the meaning of binding and loosing. This latter expression is taken from rabbinic language, where it stands primarily for the authority to make doctrinal decisions and, on the other hand, denotes a further disciplinary power, that is, the right to impose or to lift the ban. The parallelism "on earth and in heaven" implies that Peter's decisions for the Church also have validity

---

[16] Gnilka, 65.

before God—an idea that also occurs in an analogous sense in Talmudic literature. If we bear in mind the parallel to the word of the risen Jesus transmitted in John 20:23, it becomes apparent that in its core the power to bind and to loose means the authority to forgive sins, an authority that in Peter is committed to the Church (cf. Mt 18:15–18).[17]

This seems to me to be a cardinal point: at the inmost core of the new commission, which robs the forces of destruction of their power, is the grace of forgiveness. It constitutes the Church. The Church is founded upon forgiveness. Peter himself is a personal embodiment of this truth, for he is permitted to be the bearer of the keys after having stumbled, confessed and received the grace of pardon. The Church is by nature the home of forgiveness, and it is thus that chaos is banished from within her. She is held together by forgiveness, and Peter is the perpetual living reminder of this reality: she is not a communion of the perfect but a communion of sinners who need and seek forgiveness. Behind the talk of authority, God's power appears as mercy and thus as the foundation stone of the Church; in the background we hear the word of the Lord: "It is not the healthy who have need of the physician, but those who

---

[17] Gnilka, on the other hand (66), admittedly wishes to place the power to teach in the foreground. Nevertheless, I cannot agree with him when he states the opinion that "this sense [to loose sins] is out of the question in our logion." This aspect is at least implicitly stated in a disciplinary power that is binding in heaven as well as on earth.

are ill; I have not come to call the righteous, but sinners''
(Mk 2:17).

The Church can come into being only where man
finds his way to the truth about himself, and the truth
is that he needs grace. Wherever pride closes him to this
insight, man cannot find the way to Jesus. The keys to
the Kingdom of Heaven are the words of forgiveness,
which man cannot speak of himself but are granted by
God's power alone. We also understand now why this
pericope passes directly over into an announcement of
the Passion: by his death Jesus has rolled the stone over
the mouth of death, which is the power of hell, so that
from his death the power of forgiveness flows without
cease.

## 2. The question of the Petrine succession

### a. The principle of succession in general

That the primacy of Peter is recognizable in all the major
strands of the New Testament is incontestable. The real
difficulty arises when we come to the second question:
Can the idea of a Petrine succession be justified? Even
more difficult is the third question that is bound up with
it: Can the Petrine succession of Rome be credibly sub-
stantiated? Concerning the first question, we must first
of all note that there is no explicit statement regarding
the Petrine succession in the New Testament. This is
not surprising, since neither the Gospels nor the chief

Pauline epistles address the problem of a postapostolic Church—which, by the way, must be mentioned as a sign of the Gospels' fidelity to tradition. Indirectly, however, this problem can be detected in the Gospels once we admit the principle of form critical method according to which only what was considered in the respective spheres of tradition as somehow meaningful for the present was preserved in writing as such. This would mean, for example, that toward the end of the first century, when Peter was long dead, John regarded the former's primacy, not as a thing of the past, but as a present reality for the Church. For many even believe—though perhaps with a little too much imagination—that they have good grounds for interpreting the "competition" between Peter and the beloved disciple as an echo of the tensions between Rome's claim to primacy and the sense of dignity possessed by the Churches of Asia Minor. This would certainly be a very early and, in addition, inner-biblical proof that Rome was seen as continuing the Petrine line; but we should in no case rely on such uncertain hypotheses. The fundamental idea, however, does seem to me correct, namely, that the traditions of the New Testament never reflect an interest of purely historical curiosity but are bearers of present reality and in that sense constantly rescue things from the mere past, without blurring the special status of the origin.

Moreover, even scholars who deny the principle itself have propounded hypotheses of succession. O. Cull-

mann, for example, objects in a very clear-cut fashion
to the idea of succession, yet he believes that he can
show that Peter was replaced by James and that this latter assumed the primacy of the erstwhile first apostle.[18]
Bultmann believes that he is correct in concluding from
the mention of the three pillars in Galatians 2:9 that the
course of development led away from a personal to a
collegial leadership and that a college entered upon the
succession of Peter.[19] We have no need to discuss these
hypotheses and others like them; their foundation is
weak enough. Nevertheless, they do show that it is impossible to avoid the idea of succession once the word
transmitted in Scripture is considered to be a sphere
open to the future. In those writings of the New Testament that stand on the cusp of the second generation
or else already belong to it—especially in the Acts of
the Apostles and in the Pastoral Letters—the principle
of succession does in fact take on concrete shape. The
Protestant notion that the "succession" consists solely in
the word as such, but not in any "structures", is proved
to be anachronistic in light of what in actual fact is the
form of tradition in the New Testament. The word is
tied to the witness, who guarantees it an unambiguous
sense, which it does not possess as a mere word floating
in isolation. But the witness is not an individual who
stands independently on his own. He is no more a wit-

[18] See n. 2 above.
[19] *Die Geschichte der synoptischen Tradition*, 2d ed. (1981), 147–51; cf.
Gnilka, 56.

ness by virtue of himself and of his own powers of memory than Peter can be the rock by his own strength. He is not a witness as "flesh and blood" but as one who is linked to the Pneuma, the Paraclete who authenticates the truth and opens up the memory and, in his turn, binds the witness to Christ. For the Paraclete does not speak of himself, but he takes from "what is his" (that is, from what is Christ's: Jn 16:13).

This binding of the witness to the Pneuma and to his mode of being—"not of himself, but what he hears" —is called "sacrament" in the language of the Church. Sacrament designates a threefold knot—word, witness, Holy Spirit and Christ—which describes the essential structure of succession in the New Testament. We can infer with certainty from the testimony of the Pastoral Letters and of the Acts of the Apostles that the apostolic generation already gave to this interconnection of person and word in the believed presence of the Spirit and of Christ the form of the laying on of hands.

## b. The Petrine succession in Rome

In opposition to the New Testament pattern of succession described above, which withdraws the word from human manipulation precisely by binding witnesses into its service, there arose very early on an intellectual and anti-institutional model known historically by the name of Gnosis, which made the free interpretation and speculative development of the word its principle. Before

long the appeal to individual witnesses no longer suf-
ficed to counter the intellectual claim advanced by this
tendency. It became necessary to have fixed points by
which to orient the testimony itself, and these were
found in the so-called apostolic sees, that is, in those
places where the apostles had been active. The apostolic
sees became the reference point of true communio. But
among these sees there was in turn—quite clearly in
Irenaeus of Lyons—a decisive criterion that recapitu-
lated all others: the Church of Rome, where Peter and
Paul suffered martyrdom. It was with this Church that
every community had to agree; Rome was the standard
of the authentic apostolic tradition as a whole.

Moreover, Eusebius of Caesarea organized the first
version of his ecclesiastical history in accord with the
same principle. It was to be a written record of the continuity of apostolic succession, which was concentrated
in the three Petrine sees—Rome, Antioch and Alexandria—among which Rome, as the site of Peter's martyrdom, was in turn preeminent and truly normative.[20]

This leads us to a very fundamental observation.[21]

[20] For an exhaustive account of this point, see V. Twomey, *Aposto-
likos Thronos* (Münster, 1982).

[21] It is my hope that in the not-too-distant future I will have the opportunity to develop and substantiate in greater detail the view of the
succession that I attempt to indicate in an extremely condensed form
in what follows. I owe important suggestions to several works by O.
Karrer, especially: *Um die Einheit der Christen. Die Petrusfrage* (Frankfurt am Mainz, 1953); "Apostolische Nachfolge und Primat", in:
Feiner, Trütsch and Böckle, *Fragen in der Theologie heute* (Freiburg im

The Roman primacy, or, rather, the acknowledgement
of Rome as the criterion of the right apostolic faith,
is older than the canon of the New Testament, than
"Scripture". We must be on our guard here against an
almost inevitable illusion. "Scripture" is more recent
than "the scriptures" of which it is composed. It was
still a long time before the existence of the individual
writings resulted in the "New Testament" as Scripture,
as the Bible. The assembling of the writings into a single
Scripture is more properly speaking the work of tradition, a work that began in the second century but came
to a kind of conclusion only in the fourth or fifth century. Harnack, a witness who cannot be suspected of
pro-Roman bias, has remarked in this regard that it was
only at the end of the second century, in Rome, that
a canon of the "books of the New Testament" won
recognition by the criterion of apostolicity-catholicity,
a criterion to which the other Churches also gradually
subscribed "for the sake of its intrinsic value and on
the strength of the authority of the Roman Church".
We can therefore say that Scripture became Scripture
through the tradition, which precisely in this process

Breisgau, 1957), 175–206; "Das Petrusamt in der Frühkirche", in
*Festgabe J. Lortz* (Baden-Baden, 1958), 507–25; "Die biblische und
altkirchliche Grundlage des Papsttums", in: *Lebendiges Zeugnis* (1958),
3–24. Also of importance are some of the papers in the festschrift for
O. Karrer: *Begegnung der Christen*, ed. by Roesle-Cullmann (Frankfurt
am Mainz, 1959); in particular, K. Hofstetter, "Das Petrusamt in der
Kirche des 1. und 2. Jahrhunderts", 361–72.

included the *potentior principalitas*—the preeminent original authority—of the Roman see as a constitutive element.

Two points emerge clearly from what has just been
said. First, the principle of tradition in its sacramental
form—apostolic succession—played a constitutive role
in the existence and continuance of the Church. Without this principle, it is impossible to conceive of a New
Testament at all, so that we are caught in a contradiction when we affirm the one while wanting to deny
the other. Furthermore, we have seen that in Rome the
traditional series of bishops was from the very beginning recorded as a line of successors. We can add that
Rome and Antioch were conscious of succeeding to the
mission of Peter and that early on Alexandria was admitted into the circle of Petrine sees as the city where
Peter's disciple Mark had been active. Having said all
that, the site of Peter's martyrdom nonetheless appears
clearly as the chief bearer of his supreme authority and
plays a preeminent role in the formation of tradition—
which is constitutive of the Church—and thus in the
genesis of the New Testament as Bible; Rome is one of
the indispensable internal and external conditions of its
possibility. It would be exciting to trace the influence
on this process of the idea that the mission of Jerusalem
had passed over to Rome, which explains why at first
Jerusalem was not only not a ''patriarchal see'' but not
even a metropolis: Jerusalem was now located in Rome,
and since Peter's departure from that city, its primacy

had been transferred to the capital of the pagan world.[22]
But to consider this in detail would lead us too far afield
for the moment. The essential point, in my opinion, has
already become plain: the martyrdom of Peter in Rome
fixes the place where his function continues. The awareness of this fact can be detected as early as the first century in the Letter of Clement, even though it developed
but slowly in all its particulars.

### 3. Concluding reflections

We shall break off at this point, for the chief goal of our
considerations has been attained. We have seen that the
New Testament as a whole strikingly demonstrates the
primacy of Peter; we have seen that the formative development of tradition and of the Church supposed the
continuation of Peter's authority in Rome as an intrinsic condition. The Roman primacy is not an invention
of the popes, but an essential element of ecclesial unity
that goes back to the Lord and was developed faithfully
in the nascent Church.

But the New Testament shows us more than the formal aspect of a structure; it also reveals to us the inward
nature of this structure. It does not merely furnish proof
texts, it is a permanent criterion and task. It depicts the
tension between *skandalon* and rock; in the very disproportion between man's capacity and God's sovereign

---

[22] Cf. Hofstetter.

disposition, it reveals God to be the one who truly acts and is present. If in the course of history the attribution of such authority to men could repeatedly engender the not entirely unfounded suspicion of human arrogation of power, not only the promise of the New Testament but also the trajectory of that history itself prove the opposite. The men in question are so glaringly, so blatantly unequal to this function that the very empowerment of man to be the rock makes evident how little it is they who sustain the Church but God alone who does so, who does so more in spite of men than through them. The mystery of the Cross is perhaps nowhere so palpably present as in the primacy as a reality of Church history. That its center is forgiveness is both its intrinsic condition and the sign of the distinctive character of God's power. Every single biblical logion about the primacy thus remains from generation to generation a signpost and a norm, to which we must ceaselessly resubmit ourselves. When the Church adheres to these words in faith, she is not being triumphalistic but humbly recognizing in wonder and thanksgiving the victory of God over and through human weakness. Whoever deprives these words of their force for fear of triumphalism or of human usurpation of authority does not proclaim that God is greater but diminishes him, since God demonstrates the power of his love, and thus remains faithful to the law of the history of salvation, precisely in the paradox of human impotence. For with the same realism with which we declare today the sins of the popes and their disproportion to the magnitude of their commission, we must also acknowledge that Peter has repeatedly stood as the rock against ideologies, against the dissolution of the word into the plausibilities of a given time, against subjection to the powers of this world.

When we see this in the facts of history, we are not celebrating men but praising the Lord, who does not abandon the Church and who desired to manifest that he is the rock through Peter, the little stumbling stone: "flesh and blood" do not save, but the Lord saves through those who are of flesh and blood. To deny this truth is not a plus of faith, not a plus of humility, but is to shrink from the humility that recognizes God as he is. Therefore the Petrine promise and its historical embodiment in Rome remain at the deepest level an ever-renewed motive for joy: the powers of hell will not prevail against it . . .

# III

# The Universal Church
# and the Particular Church:
# The Task of the Bishop

How, then, shall the Church actually live and be structured in the concrete so as to conform to the will of the Lord? This is the question that confronts us with commanding urgency in the wake of our reflections so far. We can give to this question a very simple answer, which, however, holds in store the full wealth and thus the full complexity of whatever is truly simple. We can respond, that is, that the Church came into being when the Lord had given his body and his blood under the forms of bread and wine, whereupon he said, "Do this in memory of me."

It follows that the Church is the answer to this commission, which is an authority and an accompanying responsibility. The Church is Eucharist. This implies that the Church has her source in death and resurrection: Jesus' reference to giving up his body would have remained idle talk if his words had not really anticipated the real act of giving it up on the Cross, whereas the real enactment of these words in a sacramental memorial would be a cult of the dead, a portion of our mourning over the omnipotence of death, if the Resurrection had not transformed this body into a "life-giving spirit" (1 Cor 15:45).

But in the general line of development of the New Testament, we can perceive a second answer, which is concentrated in the name of the Church—*ecclesia*. The Church is accordingly the gathering of men from the four corners of the earth and their purification for God. Together, the two answers describe the essence of the Church and thus introduce us into her practical dimension; both answers can be summed up in the one statement that the Church is the dynamic process of horizontal and vertical unification. It is vertical unification, which brings about the union of man with the triune love of God, thus also integrating man in and with himself. But because the Church takes man to the point toward which his entire being gravitates, she automatically becomes horizontal unification as well: only by the impulse power of vertical unification can horizontal unification, by which I mean the coming together of divided humanity, also successfully take place. The Fathers summed up these two aspects—Eucharist and gathering—in the word *communio*, which is once more returning to favor today. The Church is communion; she is the communion of the Word and Body of Christ and is thus communion among men, who by means of this communion that brings them together from above and from within are made *one* people, indeed, one Body.

## 1. Eucharistic ecclesiology and episcopal office

We must now attempt to unfold this programmatic answer in concrete terms. Let us start from the fact that the Church is effectively realized in the eucharistic celebration, in which the word of preaching likewise becomes present. This fact involves first the local aspect: the Eucharist is celebrated in a concrete place together with the men who live in it. It is here that the event of gathering begins. Hence, the Church is not a club of friends or a leisure association that brings together men with the same likes and related interests. God's call is meant for all who are in this place; the Church is by her nature public. From the outset the Church has refused to understand herself on the same level as private cultic associations or other groups having private status. Had she done so, she would have enjoyed the full protection of Roman law, which allowed a great deal of room to the sphere of organizations of private right. But the Church wanted to be as public as the state itself, since she is the new people to which all are called.[1] For this reason, all who become believers in one locality have their place in the same Eucharist: rich and poor, educated and unlettered, Greeks, Jews,

[1] Using Scripture and the Fathers, E. Peterson has forcefully underlined this public character of the Church in: *Theologische Traktate* (Munich, 1951).

barbarians, men and women—wherever the Lord calls, these distinctions cease to count (Gal 3:28).

It is only with this in mind that we can understand why Ignatius of Antioch would insist so much that there can be only one episcopal office in a given place and why he so emphatically linked membership in the Church to communion with the bishop. He was defending the public character and the unity of the faith against every group spirit, against division into races and classes. Right from the beginning, the Gospel of Jesus Christ equally excludes racism and class warfare on principle. One bishop in one place stands for the fact that the Church is one for all, because God is one for all. In this sense the Church always faces an immense task of reconciliation; she is not Church if she does not bring together those who—from the point of view of their sensibilities—do not suit one another and have no sympathy for one another. Only the love of him who died for all can be the basis of this reconciliation, indeed, it *must* be the basis of such reconciliation. The Letter to the Ephesians sees the profoundest significance of the death of Christ in the fact that he has torn down "the dividing wall of enmity" (2:14). By his shed blood, Christ is "our peace" (2:13f.).

These are eucharistic formulations that contain a demanding realism: one cannot benefit from the "blood shed for many" by withdrawing to the "few". In this sense, the "monarchical episcopate" taught by Ignatius of Antioch irrevocably remains an essential structure of the Church, being as it is a precise exegesis of a crucially important reality: the Eucharist is public; it is the Eucharist of the whole Church, of the one Christ. Therefore no one may rightfully pick out "his own" Eucharist. The reconciliation with God that the Eucharist offers always demands reconciliation with one's brother as a prior condition (Mt 5:23f.). The eucharistic nature of the Church pointed first to the local gathering; at the same time we recognized that the episcopal office is an essential component of the Eucharist—as a service to the unity that follows necessarily from the character of the Eucharist as sacrifice and reconciliation. A Church understood eucharistically is a Church constituted episcopally.

We must now attempt a further step. The rediscovery of the eucharistic character of the Church has led in recent times to a strong emphasis on the principle of the local Church. Orthodox theologians have contrasted the eucharistic ecclesiology of the East, which they hold up as the authentic model of the Church, to the centralistic ecclesiology of Rome.[2] In every local Church, they maintain, the whole mystery of the

[2] Cf. N. Afanasieff et al., *La Primauté de Pierre dans l'Église orthodoxe* (Neuchâtel, 1960); idem, *L'Église du Saint-Esprit* (Paris, 1975); J. Zizioulas, *L'Être ecclésial* (Geneva, 1981); St. Charkianakis, Περὶ τὸ ἀλάθητον τῆς ἐκκλησίας ἐν τῇ ὀρθοδόξῳ θεολογίᾳ, (Athens, 1985); a mediating position is found in D. Papandreou, "La Communion ecclésiale: Un Point de vue orthodoxe", in: *Kanon. Jahrbuch der Gesellschaft für die Ostkirchen* 8 (Vienna, 1987), 15–22.

Church is present when the Eucharist is celebrated, because Christ is wholly present; there is thus nothing more to be added. Given this premise, the inference is drawn that the idea of a Petrine office is contradictory; it resorts to a worldly pattern of unity that is opposed to the sacramental unity represented in the Church's eucharistic constitution. Of course, this modern Orthodox eucharistic ecclesiology is not defined in purely "local" terms, since the point from which it is constructed is the bishop, not the place as such. If one considers this fact, it becomes obvious that for the Orthodox tradition the mere celebration of the liturgical act in the given locality does not suffice to constitute the Church; a complementary principle is needed.

The questions that are left open on this score help us to comprehend why for some time new variants of the idea, which attempt to bring it to its final logical conclusion, have developed through the fusion of Protestant, Orthodox and Catholic elements. If Orthodoxy starts from the bishop and from the eucharistic community over which he presides, the point on which the Reformed position is built is the Word: the Word of God gathers men and creates "community". The proclamation of the Gospel produces—so they say—congregation, and this congregation is the "Church". In other words, the Church as institution has in this view no properly theological status; only the community has theological significance, because what matters is the Word alone.[3] This notion of community is usually associated with the logion of Jesus in Matthew's Gospel, "Wherever two or three are gathered in my name, there I am in their midst" (18:20). One could almost say that for many this saying has replaced the logion about the rock, about the power of the keys, as the word that founds the Church and defines her essence.

The idea, then, is that assembling in the name of Jesus itself produces the Church; it is the act—independent of all institutions—in which the Church is born ever anew. The Church is not conceived episcopally but congregationally. It is now no longer necessary to fall back on the exclusivity of the Word; rather the conclusion is drawn from the above-mentioned principle that the assembly that has become an ecclesial community in this way holds all the powers of the Church, including, therefore, the power to celebrate the Eucharist. The Church comes into being, according to the popular expression, "from below"; she constitutes herself. But this approach inevitably destroys the public nature and the all-embracing reconciliatory character of the Church, both of which are represented in the episcopal principle and result from the essence of the Eucharist. The Church becomes a group held together by her inter-

---

[3] Cf. G. Gloege, "Gemeinde", in: *RGG* 2:1325-29. It goes without saying that the individual conceptions of Church and community among Reformed thinkers are manifold and diverse; nevertheless, the basic tendency does seem to me to be indicated by what is said above.

nal agreement, whereas her catholic dimension crumbles away. The Lord's word concerning the two or three who gather in his name must not be isolated; it is not a definitive and exhaustive statement of the whole of the Church's reality. The assembly, even the informal togetherness of prayer groups, has an important role in the Church. But as a constitutive principle of the Church, these things are not sufficient.

It is for such reasons that the Synod of 1985 once again drew attention to *communio* as the guiding idea for understanding the Church and thus called for a deepening of eucharistic ecclesiology wherein the various roles of pope, bishop, priest and layman are rightly contemplated together in the light of the sacrament of the Lord's Body. Endeavors in this direction are also to a large extent under way. A first step suggests itself with comparative ease. The Church is Eucharist, as we said. This can also be translated into the statement that the Church is communion, communion with the whole Body of Christ. Expressed in different terms: In the Eucharist I can never demand communion with Jesus alone. He has given himself a Body. Whoever receives him in Communion necessarily communicates with all his brothers and sisters who have become members of the one Body. *Communio* includes the dimension of catholicity by virtue of the range of the mystery of Christ. *Communio* is catholic, or it simply does not exist at all.

## 2. Structures of the universal Church
### in eucharistic ecclesiology

But how is the foregoing expressed when it is carried out in practice? This question necessarily takes us back once more to the ancient Church. Anyone who becomes acquainted with her as she lives out her life sees immediately that the ancient Church never consisted in a static juxtaposition of local Churches. Catholicity, concretely realized in many forms, belongs to her essence from the very outset. In the apostolic period it is above all the figure of the apostle itself that stands outside the scope of the local principle. The apostle is not the bishop of a community but rather a missionary for the whole Church. The figure of the apostle is the strongest refutation of every purely local conception of the Church. He expresses in his person the universal Church; he is her representative, and no local Church can claim him for herself alone. Paul carried out this function of unity by means of his letters and a network of messengers. These letters are an exercise of his catholic ministry of unity, which can be accounted for only by the apostle's authority in the Church universal. If one considers the lists of salutations in the epistles, one can further observe how mobile ancient society was; we meet Paul's friends now here, now there. For them being Christian meant belonging to a developing divine convocation that was one and the same wherever they found it.

Whenever I study the hypotheses according to which James, or a college, or simply the community itself, entered upon the succession of Peter, I am always amazed that so far it has not occurred to anyone to ascribe the Petrine succession to Paul, though he himself says in the Letter to the Galatians, "I am entrusted with the gospel for the uncircumcised as Peter with the gospel for the circumcised" (2:7). Quite apart from the fact that this text unequivocally rules out the replacement of Peter by James or by a college, as some have deduced from the same Letter to the Galatians, one might infer that Paul assumed the primacy over the Gentiles without partners. But in reality the text is referring to a distribution of missionary sectors, which became obsolete precisely in the measure that Paul's fundamental intuition, which abolished the distinction between Jewish and Gentile Christians, won the day. Peter, as the data of the New Testament as a whole demonstrate, remained the clamp that held Jewish and Gentile Christianity together, and this mission for the good of the whole Church was the concrete application of the special commission conferred upon him by the Lord. But at the same time one can say that, by reason of his mission, Paul exercised a sort of primacy over the Gentile Christians, just as James occupied a position of leadership over the entirety of Jewish Christianity.

Let us return to our question. In the apostolic period, the catholic element in the Church's structure is obvious; the so-called Catholic Epistles likewise extend and confirm it. One can even say that the ministry concerned with the universal Church enjoys such a clear precedence over local offices that the concrete physiognomy of the latter is still overshadowed in the chief Pauline letters.[4] It must be mentioned that the prophetic rank, invested with an equally supralocal mission, was active alongside the apostles. Still, these prophets are always designated in the Didachē as "your high priests" (13, 3). Only when we have grasped the meaning of this statement can we fully comprehend the import of the formula that the bishops are the successors of the apostles. In the initial phase, their position as bearers of responsibility for the local Churches is clearly subordinate to the catholic authority of the apostles. The fact that in the difficult formative process of the postapostolic Church the place of the apostles was also finally adjudged to them implies that they now assumed a responsibility whose scope transcended the local principle. It means that the catholic and missionary flame must not be extinguished even in this new situation. The Church cannot become a static juxtaposition of essentially self-sufficient local Churches. The Church must remain "apostolic", that is to say, the dynamism of unity must also mold her structure. The epithet "successor of the apostles" removes the bishop beyond the

[4] Cf. on this point the following chapter.

purely local and makes it his responsibility to ensure that the two dimensions of *communio*—the vertical and the horizontal—remain undivided.

But how does this lack of division look in practical terms? Its principal sign is a very strong awareness of the unity of the one Church in all places, an awareness that comes to the fore spontaneously where isolationist tendencies make themselves felt. When, for example, in the fourth and fifth centuries the Donatists began to create a sort of separate African Church, which no longer wished to remain in communion with the whole *Catholica*, Optatus of Milevis reacted uncompromisingly against this drift toward "two Churches". In contrast he emphasized that communion with all the provinces was the hallmark of the true Church.[5] Augustine never tires of stating the same truth and in this way became the doctor of catholicity: "I am in the Church, whose members are all those Churches about which we know in truth from Holy Scripture that they originated and grew by the activity of the apostles. I will never give up *communio* with her, neither in Africa nor anywhere else, so help me God."[6]

Irenaeus had already stressed the same unity in the second century:

[5] Cf. J. Ratzinger, *Volk und Haus Gottes in Augustins Lehre von der Kirche* (Munich, 1954), 102–23.

[6] *Contra Cresconium* 3, 35, 39: PL 43, 517.

The Church scattered across the world carefully guards
. . . this preaching . . . and this faith, since she inhabits,
as it were, one single house and in her faith is like those
who, so to say, have one soul and one heart; she preaches,
teaches and hands on her tradition in unison as if with
a single mouth. For although different languages exist
in the world, the force of tradition is still one and the
same. Neither the Churches founded in Germany, nor
those established among the Iberians or the Celts or in
the East or in Egypt or in Libya, nor those that are found
in the center of the world, have a different tradition of
faith. Rather, just as the sun, God's creature, is one and
the same in the whole world, in like manner the light,
the preaching of the truth, also shines everywhere and
illuminates all those who wish to come to the knowledge
of the truth."[7]

What, then, were the concrete structural elements
that guaranteed this catholicity? Naturally, before speaking of the structures it is necessary to mention their content, on which the Letter to the Ephesians, for example,
insists: "One Lord, one faith, one baptism, one God and
Father" (4:5f.). This is the content that the structures
serve. We had said that membership in the communion,
that is, membership in the Church, is by its essence universal. Whoever belongs to *one* local Church belongs to
all. The consciousness of this fact gave rise to the in-

---

[7] *Ad. haer.* 1, 10, 2, ed. by A. Rousseau and L. Doutreleau, *Sources
chrétiennes* 264, (Paris, 1979), 158f.

stitution of letters of communion, which were termed *litteræ communicatoriæ*, *tesseræ*, *symbola*, *litteræ pacis* or the like, and which served to secure the unity of the *communio* and to draw clear boundaries over against the pretensions of false communions.[8] Whenever a Christian went on a journey, he carried such a proof of membership; with it he would find lodging in every Christian community around the world and, as the center of this hospitality, communion in the Body of the Lord. By means of these letters of peace, the Christian was truly at home everywhere. In order for the system to function, the bishops for their part had to keep up-to-date lists of the more important Churches around the world with which they were in communion. "This list served as a register of addresses when it was necessary to issue the passes, and, on the other side, the passes of arriving travellers were checked against this list."[9]

Here we see a very concrete way in which the bishop is the ligature of catholicity. He keeps his Church connected with the others and thus embodies the apostolic and, therefore, the catholic element of the Church. This fact is expressed in his very consecration: no community can simply give itself its own bishop. Such a radical

---

[8] Concerning this and the following point, see the fundamental article by L. Hertling, "Communio und Primat—Kirche und Papsttum in der christlichen Antike", in: *Una Sancta* 17 (1962): 91–125. (Initial publication was in *Miscellanea Historiæ Pontificiæ* [Rome, 1943] and has since then been repeatedly reissued.)

[9] Ibid., 100.

embedding in the local is incompatible with the principle of apostolicity and, hence, of universality. A deeper reality is indicated here: faith is not something we have produced ourselves but something we again and again receive from an outside source. Faith always implies the surpassing of a limit; it presupposes movement toward others and from others, which then points to the origin from *the* other, the Lord himself. The bishop is consecrated by a group of at least three neighboring bishops, who also verify that he professes the same creed.[10] But the neighboring bishops do not, of course, suffice—consider the radius that the text of Irenaeus describes; it is meant to encompass the then known ends of the earth in its span, from Germany on one side to Egypt and the Orient on the other.

Only if we carefully examine this point can we avoid a misunderstanding of *communio* ecclesiology that is rapidly gaining ground today. A one-sided contemporary interpretation of local Church tradition is thought to necessitate the conclusion that there is nothing relevant to the constitution of the Church beyond the individual local bishops. The only possible organ of the universal Church is held to be the general council, while the Church is said to be the permanent council formed by the many bishops. Hence, some have even proposed

---

[10] Cf. B. Botte, "Der Kollegialcharakter des Priester- und Bischofsamtes", in: J. Guyot (ed.), *Das apostolische Amt* (Mainz, 1961), 68–91; concerning this point, 80f.

considering the council as *the* blueprint of the Church as such.[11] This sort of ecclesiology, however, lacks the element of responsibility for the universal Church embodied in the apostle. Thus, the episcopal office itself is foreshortened, with the result that even the local Church is no longer seen in her full intrinsic breadth.

On the other hand, it is not at all easy to bring into focus the structural element that in the ancient Church extended beyond the individual bishop without immediately falling under the suspicion of a unilaterally papal reading of history. I would like to try to illustrate this structure in light of a specific instance, namely, the controversy surrounding Paul of Samosata, the bishop of Antioch, who in the year 268 was convicted of heresy by an assembly of bishops, relieved of his office and excommunicated.

The proceedings had particularly far-reaching importance, because Antioch was the place where Gentile Christianity had developed and where the name Christian had been coined. Tradition recognized Antioch as the site of Peter's missionary activity before his departure for Rome. Accordingly, Antioch was a central reference point of the *communio*. In other words, the worldwide network of *communio* had—as we have already heard—a few prominent reference points by which the surrounding local Churches took their measure. These

---

[11] See on this point J. Ratzinger, *Das neue Volk Gottes* (Düsseldorf, 1969), 147–70.

are the apostolic sees. For this reason the crisis of such a principal see was particularly momentous: What happens when a reference point itself falters? Obviously mere "neighborly help" no longer suffices in this situation. For here the whole is at stake. Consequently, while the synod of neighboring bishops can indeed resolve to depose and can choose a successor, it cannot give its decisions definitive juridical force. In this case the *Catholica* itself must take action. Accordingly, the participants of the Antiochene synod of bishops wrote at that time to the bishops of Rome and Alexandria and, through them, to the other bishops of the Catholic Church, "We were thus constrained . . . to appoint another as bishop in his stead on behalf of the Catholic Church . . . Domnus, who is outstanding in all the qualities that become a bishop. We have informed you of this so that you might write to him and receive from him the letters of communion."[12]

This implies that Domnus cannot be legitimated by the synod alone. His appointment is validated only when the bishops of Rome and Alexandria learn of his election, write to him and accept from him the κοινωνικὰ γράμματα. But the case continues. Paul of Samosata refused to return buildings dedicated to worship. Thereupon the bishops applied to the (pagan!) emperor Aurelian, who decreed that the buildings were to be handed over to "whomever the bishops of Italy

---

[12] Eusebius, *History of the Church* 7, 30, 17.

and of the city of Rome would acknowledge as lawful".[13]

The Belgian scholar B. Botte rightly concludes from this episode: "In the eyes of the pagan emperor there were not only local Churches but a catholic Church, whose unity was guaranteed by the communion of the bishops."[14] The same facts that this case study reveals for the third century can be documented for the second in the context of the controversy over the dating of Easter.[15] The Council of Nicaea, by its own declaration, was merely confirming ancient tradition when it laid down the primacies of Rome, Alexandria and Antioch and defined them as the hinges of the universal *communio*.[16] The warrant of these three sees lies in the Petrine principle, as does the basis of Rome's apostolic responsibility to be the norm of unity. Consequently, both neighborly solicitude and living relation with Rome pertain to the catholicity of a bishop as ways of giving and receiving in the great communion of the one Church.[17]

[13] Ibid., 19.

[14] Botte, 83.

[15] Cf. J. Colson, *L'Épiscopat catholique. Collégialité et primauté dans les trois premiers siècles* (Paris, 1963), 49–52.

[16] Can. 6.

[17] Helpful information on the historical functioning of the Nicene system, which included the primacy of Rome, can be found in J. Richards, *Gregor der Große. Sein Leben—seine Zeit* (Graz, 1983), esp. 224–34; English original: *Consul of God: The Life and Times of Gregory the Great* (London, Boston: Routledge & Kegan Paul, 1980).

The Protestant legal scholar R. Sohm once remarked that, in the first millennium, the Church was understood as the Body of Christ but, in the second millennium, as the juridical body of Christians.[18] In this transition from body to corporation, from Christ to Christendom, from sacrament to law, Sohm sees the real apostasy that supposedly took place at the turn of the second millennium and, in his view, first produced the Roman Catholic Church. In opposition to this we must say that, while the Church is indeed constituted primarily by sacramentality and by her communion with Christ, precisely because she is the "Body of Christ", she is corporeal and is the corporation of Christians. The two things are not mutually exclusive but, rather, mutually conditioning. Because the Church is sacramental communion in the Body of the Lord and on the basis of his Word, it is the communion of sacred law, as E. Käsemann has penetratingly shown in light of the New Testament.[19]

This "sacred law" resulting from Word and sacrament is concretely environed by various kinds of human law; throughout her history, the Church will have to apply constant care that an excess of human structures does

---

[18] On Sohm: W. Böckenförde, *Das Rechtsverständnis der neueren Kanonistik und die Kritik Rudolph Sohms*, dissertation (Münster in Westfalen, 1969).

[19] E. Käsemann, "Sätze heiligen Rechts im Neuen Testament", in: idem *Exegetische Versuche und Besinnungen* 2 (Göttingen, 1964): 69–82.

not disguise her authentic spiritual center. It is important to hold firmly that the order of unity is not one of purely human law but that unity is a key characteristic of the Church's essence, so that the juridical expression of unity in the office of Peter's successor and in the necessary dependence of the bishops both on one another and on him belongs to the core of her sacred order. Hence, the loss of this element wounds her at the point where she is most truly Church.

### 3. Consequences for the office and mission of the bishop

In all our reflections on the relationship between the universal Church and the particular Church, we have repeatedly encountered the figure of the bishop as a central element of the Church's constitution. He embodies the unity and the public character of the local Church that derive from the unity of Word and sacrament, as we have said. He is at the same time the link connecting his Church to the other local Churches: just as he answers for the unity of the Church in his territory, in his diocese, it is also incumbent upon him to mediate and constantly enliven the unity of his local Church with the entire, one Church of Jesus Christ. He must be solicitous for the catholic and apostolic dimensions of his local Church: these two elements of the Church's essence mold his office in a particular way,

but they also have an immediate connection with the
two other distinctive notes of the Church. Apostolicity
and catholicity serve unity, and without unity there is
also no holiness. This is so because without love there
is no holiness, which is realized principally in the in-
tegration of the individual and of individuals into the
reconciling love of the one Body of Jesus Christ. It
is not the perfecting of one's own self that makes one
holy but the purification of the self through its fusion
into the all-embracing love of Christ: it is the holiness
of the triune God himself.

Supposing these basic ecclesiological principles, how
are we to define more precisely the mission of the
bishop and the status of the particular Church in the universal Church? This question introduces a broad subject, for it leads us into the domain where principles
must be implemented practically in the historical situation. Although this domain always presupposes the
same foundations, it constantly confronts them with
new realities of human life and therefore constantly demands new answers. I must content myself here with
underlining a couple of general aspects.

If the bishop is to be defined essentially as a successor
of the apostles, the fundamental coordinates of his mission are determined by what Scripture says to be Jesus'
will in regard to the apostles: They are "made" that they
"might be with him", "that he might send them" and
"that they might have authority" (Mk 3:14f.). The basic prerequisite for episcopal ministry is intimate com-

munion with Jesus, being with him. The bishop must be a witness of the Resurrection, hence, he must be in contact with the risen Christ. Unless the bishop is inwardly "with" Christ, unless he is Christ's "contemporary", he becomes a mere ecclesiastical functionary, in which case he is not a witness or a successor of the apostles. To be with the Lord requires interiorization, but at the same time it also brings about participation in the dynamism of the Lord's mission. For the Lord is entirely the emissary who has come down from heaven in order to make his existence with the Father an existence with men. According to the classical categories, the episcopal office belongs to the *vita activa*, but the activity meant here finds its ordering principle in its insertion into the dynamism of the mission of Jesus Christ. The bishop's activity is thus above all to convey to men existence with Christ, and thus existence with God, and to gather them into it themselves.

If the third axis of the mission of the apostles is the authority conferred upon them to cast out evil spirits, the sense of this commission becomes clear in the present context: the arrival of the mission of Jesus heals and purifies man from within. It cleanses the "atmosphere" of the spirit in which he lives by bringing in the Spirit of Jesus, the Holy Spirit of God. To be with God through Christ's mediation and, as Christ's emissary, to bring God to men, to make them the *qahal*, the convocation of God—this is the mission of the bishop. "He who does not gather with me scatters", says Jesus (Mt 12:30; Lk 11:23): the bishop's *raison d'être* is to gather with Jesus.

A second point follows from what has been said: the bishop is the successor of the apostles, but only the bishop of Rome is the successor of a particular apostle —of Saint Peter—and is thus given responsibility for the whole Church. All the remaining bishops are successors of the *apostles* in general; they do not succeed a certain apostle but are members of the college that takes the place of the apostolic college, and this fact makes each single one of them a successor of the apostles. But this means that to be a successor is also tied to participation in the "we" formed by all the successors. The "collegial" aspect is an essential component of episcopal office and a necessary consequence of its catholic and apostolic dimensions. This collegial togetherness has assumed various forms historically and the particular modes of its implementation will also vary in the future. In the ancient Church, it had two fundamental forms, which despite all changes in matters of detail still indicate what is essential today.

First of all there is the special bond uniting the neighboring bishops of a region, who in a shared political and cultural context seek to plot a common course for their episcopal ministry. This was the origin of the synods (assemblies of bishops), which in the North Africa of

Saint Augustine's time, for example, met together twice
a year.[20] In a certain sense, it is quite legitimate to com-
pare them with today's bishops' conferences. There is,
however, a hardly minor difference: these synods had no
permanent institutional infrastructure. There were no
bureaus or permanent administrative bodies, only the
assembly taking place at the moment, in which the bishops alone—drawing on their faith and on their experience as pastors—attempted themselves to find answers
to urgent questions. This system required the personal
responsibility of each bishop as well as the search for
the symphony of faith, in which the common witness
becomes a common answer.

The second figure in which the "we" of the bishops
took form in the sphere of action consisted in their relationship to the "primacies", to the normative episcopal
sees and their occupants. In particular, this relationship
included measurement by the standard of Rome and
harmony with the testimony of faith of the successor
of Peter.[21]

---

[20] Cf. C. Vogel, "Unité de l'Église et pluralité des formes histori-
ques d'organisation ecclésiastique, du IIIᵉ au Vᵉ siècle", in: Y. Con-
gar and B. D. Dupuy (ed.), *L'Épiscopat et l'Église universelle* (Paris,
1962), 591–636; J. Colson, 39–52.

[21] The "primacies" having a Petrine foundation spring from ancient theological tradition and include the special primacy of Rome.
They are to be distinguished from the idea of the patriarchate developed in Byzantium; this notion was at first categorically refused
by Rome and was adopted for that city only with hesitation. Cf. J.

In speaking of the "we" of the bishops, however, it is necessary to add yet a further plane: this "we" extends not only synchronically but also diachronically. It follows that in the Church no generation is isolated. In the Body of Christ, death no longer works as a limit; in this Body, past, present and future interpenetrate. The bishop never represents himself alone, and he does not proclaim his own ideas; he is an emissary and, as such, is the messenger of Jesus Christ. He is guided into the heart of the message by the "we" of the Church, by which I mean the "we" of the Church of all times. A majority that formed at some juncture against the faith of the Church of all times would be no majority: the true majority in the Church reaches diachronically across the ages, and only when one listens to this plenary majority does one remain in the apostolic "we". Faith explodes the self-absolutization of individual presents; by opening them to the faith of all times, it liberates them from ideological delusion and at the same time holds open the future. To be the spokesman of this diachronic majority, of the voice of the Church that unites all epochs, is one of the chief roles of the bishop that follows from the "we"-character of his office.

Let us add briefly two further elements. The bishop represents the universal Church in relation to the local

---

Richards, 228; for a detailed and thorough treatment see A. Garuti, *Il Papa Patriarca d'occidente? Studio storico dottrinale* (Bologna, 1990).

Church and vice versa. In this way he serves unity.
He does not permit the local Church to become self-
enclosed but opens her up to the whole, so that the
life-giving forces of the charisms can flow in and out
of her. Just as he opens up the local Church to the
universal Church, he also introduces into the universal
Church the particular voice of his diocese, its particular charisms, its assets and its afflictions. Everything
belongs to everyone. Every organ is important, and the
contribution of each one is necessary for the whole. For
this reason the successor of Saint Peter must discharge
his office in such a way that it does not stifle the special
gifts of the single local Churches or compel them into
a false uniformity but, rather, allows them to play an
active part in the vital exchange of the whole. These
imperatives also apply to the bishop in his territory
and especially to the common leadership that the bishops exercise through the synod or the episcopal conference. Like the pope, the bishop and the bishops' conference ought to impose in their sphere only as much
human law as is truly needed above and beyond the
sacred law rooted in the sacramental principle. They,
too, must beware of reduction to uniformity in their
work as pastors. They, too, must hold to the rules pre-
scribed by Saint Paul: "Do not extinguish the Spirit
. . . test everything, retain what is good" (1 Th 5:19,
21). They, too, must not pursue uniformity in their pastoral planning but must leave room for the doubtless often troublesome multiplicity of God's gifts—always, of

course, under the criterion of unity of faith. No more
human forms ought to be added to this criterion than
are required for peaceable living and harmonious co-
existence.

Finally, we must not forget that the apostle is always sent "to the ends of the earth". Consequently,
the task of the bishop can never be exhausted within
the Church. The gospel is always addressed to all, so
that the successor of the apostles always has the further
responsibility to bring it into the world. This is true in
a double sense. The faith must be announced in every
new situation to those who until now have not had
the chance to recognize Christ as the redeemer of the
world. In addition, the bishop also has a responsibility
for the public affairs of this world. The state is entitled to autonomy with respect to the Church, and the
bishop must acknowledge that the state has its own reality and law. He avoids mixing faith and politics and
serves the freedom of all by refusing to allow faith to be
identified with a particular form of politics. The Gospel
prescribes certain truths and values to politics, but it
does not respond to concrete questions concerning particular political and economic issues. This "autonomy
of earthly things", of which the Second Vatican Council spoke, must be respected. It must also hold good
among the members of the Church. Only in this way
does the Church remain an open space of reconciliation among the parties; only so is she preserved from
becoming a party herself. In this sense respect for the

maturity of the laity is also an important aspect of the
episcopal ministry.

But the autonomy of earthly things is not absolute.
Referring to the experiences of Rome's imperial period,
Augustine drew attention to the fact that the boundaries between the state and the robber band become
fluid when a certain ethical minimum is no longer met.
Right is not simply produced by the state; what is in
itself wrong, such as the killing of innocent men, cannot be made right by any law. For this reason the task
of preserving the capacity to hear the voice of creation
devolves upon Christians. The bishop must struggle
to keep men from becoming deaf to the fundamental
principles that God has inscribed in every heart, in the
nature of man and of reality itself. Saint Gregory the
Great once made the beautiful remark that the bishop
must have a "nose", that is, that sense that allows him
to distinguish between positive and negative.[22] This is
true within the Church and with regard to the world.
The very respect for the proper identity of worldly laws
requires that the Church step forth as the advocate of
creation wherever its voice is shouted down in the bab-
ble of self-constructed values. The bishop will consider
himself responsible for the awakening of consciences
and for the obviation of the impression that in these
areas of fundamental concern, the Church is speaking
for herself alone. Once again, laymen are called upon

[22] *Hom. in Ezech.* 1, 11, 7: PL 76, 909 A.

in a special way to exercise their responsibility in this domain, but it is also evident that laymen and priests do not live in two separate worlds but can fulfill their task only insofar as the one faith brings them together.

All of this shows, in conclusion, that the readiness to suffer also belongs to the episcopal office. Whoever regarded this office above all as an honor or as an influential position would misunderstand its essential nature. Without the readiness to undergo suffering, this task cannot be exercised. Precisely in this way the bishop is in communion with his Lord; precisely in this way he knows himself to be a "servant of your joy" (2 Cor 1:24).

# IV

# On the Essence of the Priesthood

## *Preliminary consideration: The problems*

The Catholic model of the priesthood, which was validly defined by the Council of Trent and biblically renewed and deepened by Vatican II, entered a profound crisis after that latter Council. The great number of men who have given up the priesthood, as well as the dramatic decline in new priestly vocations in many countries, are certainly not due solely to reasons of theology. But all the other causes could not have penetrated so forcefully from without if, to many priests and young men preparing for the priesthood, this ministry had not become dubious from within. In the new intellectual openness that had arisen as a result of the Council, the old Reformation-era arguments, combined with the findings of modern exegesis, which had itself been nourished to a large extent by Reformation presuppositions, suddenly acquired an obviousness that Catholic theology did not have sufficiently well-founded answers to refute. The texts of Vatican II had indeed far exceeded Trent in their incorporation of biblical motifs, but their essential content did not go beyond the traditional framework. Hence, they were inadequate to furnish a new justification of the priesthood and to shed new light on its nature in changed circumstances. Since then, the Synod of Bishops of 1971, the texts of the International Theological Commission of the same year and an abundant theological literature[1] have considerably broadened the debate, so that it is now gradually becoming possible to harvest the fruits of this dispute and to give answers to new questions in the light of a more profound reading of the texts of the Bible.

What, then, is the nature of these questions? Their starting point is an observation regarding terminology: the nascent Church named her developing ministries, not with a sacral, but with a profane vocabulary.[2] It thus becomes impossible to recognize any continuity between these offices and the priesthood of the Mosaic law. In addition, throughout a long period of time these offices were little defined and occurred under a great variety of titles and forms; it is only toward the end of the first century that a stable pattern crystallized, though even then this pattern continued to allow variations.

---

[1] Cf. *Bischofssynode 1971*, preface by Cardinal J. Höffner, commentary by H. U. von Balthasar (Einsiedeln, 1972); Intern. Theologenkommission, *Priesterdienst* (Einsiedeln, 1972). For further literature, I refer to J. Galot, *Theology of the Priesthood* (Washington, 1984); G. Greshake, *Priestersein,* expanded edition (Freiburg im Breisgau, 1991); *Résurrection: Cahiers théologiques 61: Le sacerdoce apostolique* (Desclée, 1979).

[2] This opinion, which is current in modern exegesis, has recently been energetically contested—especially in relation to the semantic field *Diakonia, diakonein*, etc.—by J. N. Collins, *Διακινεῖν and Associated Vocabulary in Early Christian Tradition*, doctoral thesis (University of London, 1976).

Above all there is no sign that these offices were em-
powered for cultic worship: nowhere are they explicitly
connected with the celebration of the Eucharist. Indeed,
their content appears to be principally the proclamation
of the Gospel and, in second place, the ministry of love
among Christians, along with functions of a more practical sort within the community.

All of these data arouse the impression that these offices were seen, not sacrally but in purely functional
terms, that is, that they were administered entirely according to considerations of practical utility. In the postconciliar period, these observations wedded themselves
quite naturally with the theory of Christianity as the
desacralization of the world, which was based upon the
Barthian and Bonhoefferian thesis of the opposition between faith and religion, hence, of the areligious character of Christianity. The emphatic affirmation of the
Letter to the Hebrews that Jesus suffered his Passion
outside the gates of the city and in consequence sum-
mons us to come out to him (Heb 13:12f.) now became
a symbol: the Cross has rent the veil of the temple, the
new altar stands in the midst of the world, the new sacrifice is not a cultic event but an entirely profane death.
The Cross thus appears as a new and revolutionary interpretation of the only meaning that cultic worship
can still have: everyday love amidst the profanity of the
world is supposedly the sole liturgy that conforms to this
origin.

This kind of reasoning, which resulted from a com-

bination of modern Protestant theology and the findings of exegesis, proves on closer inspection to be the
fruit of the fundamental hermeneutical options developed in the Reformation of the sixteenth century. The
central point of these options was a reading of the Bible
based on the dialectical opposition of law and promise,
of priest and prophet, of cult and promise. The mutually coordinated categories of law, priest and cult were
classified as the negative aspect of the history of salvation: the law, it was maintained, leads man to self-
righteousness; cultic worship presupposes the error that
man stands on a sort of equal footing with God and can
establish a relationship of justice between himself and
God by offering certain gifts; priesthood, on this reading, is, so to say, the institutional expression and the permanent instrument of this perverted relationship with
God.

The essence of the gospel, which is said to appear
at its clearest particularly in the major Pauline epistles,
would then be the overcoming of this structure raised by
man's destructive self-righteousness. The new relationship to God rests entirely on promise and grace, and
it finds expression in the figure of the prophet, who
is accordingly construed as strictly opposed to the cult
and the priesthood. Catholicism appeared to Luther as
the sacrilegious reinstatement of the cult, of sacrifice,
priesthood and law. He therefore saw it as the negation
of grace, as apostasy from the gospel, as a return behind
Christ to Moses. This hermeneutical option of Luther

has molded modern critical exegesis from its very foundation; the antithesis between cult and the proclamation of the gospel, between priest and prophet, is the pervasive influence that shapes its judgments and interpretations.

The above-mentioned philological observations seemed for all intents and purposes to furnish conclusive proof of this system of categories. It is thus comprehensible that Catholic theologians, to whom this prehistory, together with the problematic nature of the options it involved, was unknown, lost their footing when suddenly confronted with the scientific claim of modern exegesis. It appeared indisputably clear that the teaching of Trent concerning the priesthood had been formulated on false assumptions and that even Vatican II had not yet found the courage to lead the exodus from this misguided history. On the other hand, the inner tendency of the Council seemingly required that we now finally do what it had not dared to do itself: to abandon the ancient conceptions of cult and priesthood and to seek a Church at once biblical and modern that would resolutely take up the challenge of the profane world and would be organized solely according to functional considerations.

Now, in saying all this, we must, to be fair, mention that there were countertendencies even at the time of the Reformation, even within Lutheranism and Luther's own works. In spite of everything, ordination was soon understood as much more than a purely functional de-

cree that could be revoked at any moment but was conceived as having at least a certain analogy to a sacrament. Its connection with the celebration of the Eucharist quickly reemerged, and it was even seen once
more that the Eucharist and preaching are not to be dis-
joined. In any case, the ideas about the radically profane
nature of Christianity and the nonreligious character of
faith first originate in a twentieth-century constellation;
for Luther these theories would still have been thoroughly inconceivable and unacceptable. Accordingly, it
was precisely the branch of Protestantism tracing itself
back to Luther that also developed a strong cultic tradition, whose deepening in the liturgical spring of the
twentieth century made possible fruitful ecumenical encounters.[3] The legitimate questions of the Reformation
were duly registered in this movement, but at the same
time the eye for the perennial values of catholicity was
gradually resharpened. The "catholic" strand of Protestant theology consequently helped most to overcome
the unilateral emphases of certain modern interpretations of the Bible.

[3] Instructive in this regard are W. Birnbaum, *Das Kultusproblem
und die liturgischen Bewegungen des 20. Jahrhunderts,* vol. 1: *Die deutsche
katholische liturgische Bewegung* (Tübingen, 1966); vol. 2: *Die deutsche
evangelische liturgische Bewegung* (Tübingen, 1970). On the ecumenical dispute: K. Lehmann and W. Pannenberg (ed.), *Lehrverurteilungen-
kirchentrennend?* 1–3 (Freiburg and Göttingen, 1986–1990).

### 1. The foundation of ministerial office in the New Testament: Apostleship as participation in the mission of Christ

The point, then, is to recognize the novelty of the New Testament and to understand the gospel as gospel, while at the same time acquiring the proper understanding of the unity of the Old and New Covenant, of the unity of God's action. For precisely in their newness Christ's message and work simultaneously fulfill everything that had preceded and make visible the unifying center of God's history with us. When we inquire about the center of the New Testament, we come immediately to Christ himself. What is new about it is not, strictly speaking, ideas—the novelty is a person: God who becomes man and draws man to himself.

For this reason the point of departure for our inquiry must lie in Christology. It is not surprising that the liberal era interpreted Christ entirely in terms of its assumptions, which are a nineteenth-century mirror image of the categories we have just described. Jesus opposed pure ethical experience to a religion distorted by ritual and set the individual against the collective: such was the liberal claim. Jesus appears as the great ethical teacher who frees man from the constraints of cultic ritual and places him directly before God with his personal conscience.[4] In the second half of our century, such notions formed an alliance with Marxist ideas: Christ now appears as the revolutionary of love, who pits himself against the enslaving power of institutions and dies in combat against them (especially against the priesthood). He is portrayed as the pioneering champion of the liberation of the poor whose goal is to establish the "kingdom", that is, the new society of free and equal men.[5]

The figure of Jesus as it is presented to us in the Bible, however, looks quite different. We cannot, of course, develop a comprehensive Christology here. For us the decisive aspect consists in Jesus' claim to have a direct mission from God, hence, to represent God's authority concretely in his person. In all the Gospels, he appears as the bearer of a power received from God (Mt 7:29, 21:23; Mk 1:27, 11:28; Lk 20:2, 24:19, et passim). He announces a message that he does not fabricate himself, he is "sent" on a mission that is assigned him by the Father. John has developed this idea of mission with particular clarity, but in so doing he only confirms and elucidates an aspect that also plays a central role in the Synoptics.

The paradox of Jesus' mission is expressed most plainly in the Johannine formula interpreted so profoundly by Augustine: "My doctrine is not mine"

---

[4] Typical of this position is A. von Harnack, *Das Wesen des Christentums* (1900; new impression, Stuttgart, 1950).

[5] Cf., for example, L. Boff, *Jesus Cristo Libertador* (Petrópolis, 1972).

(7:16). Jesus has nothing of his own aside from the Father. He himself is involved in his doctrine: thus, he is saying that precisely what is most intimately his own—his self—is that which is altogether not his own. What is his is what is not his; nothing stands next to the Father, everything is entirely from him and for him. But precisely by this expropriation of himself, Jesus is totally one with the Father. His selflessness is his true accreditation: it gives him ultimate authority, because it becomes a pure transparency that makes God himself present.

Let us leave aside the fact that the mystery of the Trinity appears through this total entrustment of the "I" to the "thou", and the mutual infolding of them that is its result, and at the same time becomes the model of our existence. What is important for us in this context is Jesus' creation of the new figure of the Twelve, which after the Resurrection then passes over into the office of the apostles—of those who have been sent. Jesus confers his power upon the apostles and thereby makes their office strictly parallel to his own mission. "He who receives you receives me", he says to the Twelve (Mt 10:40; cf. Lk 10:16; Jn 13:20).

A rabbinic saying comes to mind: "A man's envoy is like the man himself." Pertinent here is the whole string of texts in which Jesus transmits his own "power" (authority) to the disciples: Matthew 9:8; 10:1; 21:23; Mark 6:7; 13:34; Luke 4:6; 9:1; 10:19. For its part, the Fourth Gospel goes on to complete in especially clear terms the parallelism between the form of Jesus' mission and the form of the mission of the apostles: "As the Father has sent me, so I send you" (13:20; 17:18; 20:21).[6]

The weight of this statement first becomes evident when we recall what we have just heard regarding the structure of Jesus' mission—regarding the fact that his whole being is mission and relationship. This point allows us to understand the significance of the following parallelism:

The Son can do nothing of himself (Jn 5:19, 30).

Without me you can do nothing (Jn 15:5).

This "nothing" that the disciples share with Jesus expresses at once the power and the impotence of the apostolic office. On their own, by the force of their own understanding, knowledge and will, they cannot do anything they are meant to do as apostles. How could they possibly say "I forgive you your sins"? How could they conceivably say "This is my body" or impose their hands and pronounce the words "Receive the Holy Spirit"? Nothing that makes up the activity of the apostles is the product of their own capabilities. But it is precisely in having "nothing" to call their own that their communion with Jesus consists, since Jesus is also entirely from the Father, has being only through

    [6] Cf. K. H. Schelkle, *Jüngerschaft und Apostelamt* (Freiburg, 1957).

him and in him and would not exist at all if he were not a continual coming forth from and self-return to the Father. Having "nothing" of their own draws the apostles into communion of mission with Christ. This service, in which we are made the entire property of another, this giving of what does not come from us, is called sacrament in the language of the Church.

This is precisely what we mean when we call the ordination of priests a sacrament: ordination is not about the development of one's own powers and gifts. It is not the appointment of a man as a functionary because he is especially good at it, or because it suits him, or simply because it strikes him as a good way to earn his bread; it is not a question of a job in which someone secures his own livelihood by his own abilities, perhaps in order to rise later to something better.

Sacrament means: I give what I myself cannot give; I do something that is not my work; I am on a mission and have become the bearer of that which another has committed to my charge. Consequently, it is also impossible for anyone to declare himself a priest or for a community to make someone a priest by its own *fiat*. One can receive what is God's only from the sacrament, by entering into the mission that makes me the messenger and instrument of another. Of course, this very self-expropriation for the other, this leave-taking from oneself, this self-dispossession and selflessness that are essential to the priestly ministry can lead to authentic human maturity and fulfillment. For in this movement away from self we are conformed to the mystery of the Trinity; hence, the *imago Dei* is consummated, and the fundamental pattern according to which we were created is brought to new life. Because we have been created in the image of the Trinity, the deepest truth about each man is that only he who loses himself can find himself.

But in saying this we have already got slightly ahead of ourselves. Nevertheless, we have made a fundamentally important discovery. According to the Gospels, Christ himself conferred both the structure of his mission and his existence as mission on the apostles, to whom he entrusts his full authority, thereby binding them to it. This bond to the Lord, which enables man to do what he cannot do but what the Lord does, is synonymous with the sacramental structure. In this respect, the sacramental quality of the new mode of mission originating from Christ reaches back into the very core of the Christian message, to which it indeed belongs. At the same time it has become evident that we are dealing with an entirely new type of ministry that cannot be derived from the Old Testament but can be accounted for solely in christological terms. The sacramental ministerial office of the Church is the expression of the newness of Jesus Christ that also keeps this novelty present across the temporal span of history.

## 2. The apostolic succession

After this brief glance at the christological starting point and the christological center of the new ministry that Jesus Christ created by the authority of his mission, we must now face the following question: How was this ministry picked up in the apostolic period? And, above all, what does the transition from the apostolic to the postapostolic era look like: What image of the *successio apostolorum*, which alongside the christological foundation constitutes the second mainstay of the Catholic doctrine of the New Covenant priesthood, is reflected in the mirror of the New Testament?

We can be very brief regarding the first point, which concerns the continuation in the apostolic period of what was initiated with Christ, for the Gospel records carry a double load of history. On the one hand, they are traditional accounts of what took place at the beginning —in the activity of Jesus. On the other hand, they also mirror what emerged from that beginning. Thus, what they narrate touching the apostolic office is not only evidence of the historical inception but also reflects the interpretation of the apostolic office in the developing Church.

But in addition we have the whole weighty testimony of Saint Paul, who in his letters permits us to observe apostleship in action, so to speak. The most important passage seems to me to be found in the well-nigh im-

ploring appeal in the Second Letter to the Corinthians: "We are ambassadors in Christ's stead, so that it is
as though God is admonishing through us. In Christ's
stead we pray: Be reconciled with God" (2 Cor 5:20).
This text displays quite plainly that representative and
missionary character of the apostolic ministry that we
have just come to understand as the essence of a "sacrament"; the God-given authority originating precisely in
self-dispossession, in not speaking in one's own name,
emerges clearly in this passage. This authority moves
Paul to say somewhat later: "We are God's deacons"
(6:4). But this passage also briefly summarizes the content of the apostolic ministry, which Paul calls the "ministry of reconciliation" (5:18)—of reconciliation with
God, which springs from the Cross of Christ and therefore also has "sacramental" character.

Paul thus presupposes that by his own doing man lives
in "estrangement" (Eph 2:12) and that only through
contact with the crucified love of Jesus can this alienation of man from God and from his own nature be overcome, so that man may be "reconciled". The Cross is
—as 2 Corinthians 5 clearly shows—of crucial importance in this event of reconciliation. Since as a historical
happening it belongs to the past, it can be appropriated
only "sacramentally", though Paul does not explain in
detail here how this takes place. However, when we
listen to 1 Corinthians, we perceive that baptism and
the Eucharist, which are inseparable from the word of
preaching that produces faith and thus brings us to new

birth, are essential for this event. Accordingly, it also becomes quite clear in Paul that the "sacramental" authority of the apostolate is a specific ministry and in no wise describes Christian life as a whole, though many have wanted to draw this conclusion from the fact that the Twelve represent at the same time the future office and the Church as a whole.

The specific quality of the apostolic mission in the sense just described shines out when Paul says in the First Letter to the Corinthians: "So let us be considered as servants of Christ and as administrators of the mysteries of God" (4:1). In the very same First Letter to the Corinthians, moreover, the authority of the apostle in relation to the community also comes to light, as, for example, when Paul asks: "Shall I come to you with the rod or in love with the spirit of mildness?" (4:21). The apostle who inflicts excommunication "to rescue the spirit on the day of the Lord" (5:5) and who, if the need arises, is also ready to "come with the rod", has nothing to do with the pneumatic anarchy that in our day a number of theologians have suddenly claimed to read as the ideal model of the Church in the very same First Letter to the Corinthians.[7]

The Pauline epistles thus corroborate and define more precisely what we had inferred from the Gospels: the christologically founded office of "ministers of the New

[7] Cf. F. W. Maier, *Paulus als Kirchengründer und kirchlicher Organisator* (Würzburg, 1961), esp. the summary on page 78.

Covenant" (2 Cor 3:6), which as such has to be understood sacramentally. They show us the apostle as the bearer of a Christ-given authority vis-à-vis the community. The apostle's position vis-à-vis the community continues that of Christ vis-à-vis the world and the Church. In other words, it carries forward that dialogical structure that pertains to the essence of revelation. Faith is not something we excogitate ourselves; man does not make himself a Christian by reflection or ethical achievement. He always becomes a Christian from outside: by means of a gift that can only come to him from another, through the "thou" of Christ, in whom the "thou" of God encounters him. Whenever this opposition, which expresses the fact that grace comes from outside us, disappears, the essential structure of Christianity is destroyed. A community that is its own author is no longer an image of the dialogical mystery of revelation and of the gift of grace that always comes from without and can be attained only in receiving. The opposition of gift and receiver pertains to every sacrament; but it also pertains to the Word of God. Faith, in fact, does not come from reading but from hearing; the word of proclamation, in which I am addressed by another, belongs to the structure of the act of faith.

But we must now make the next step and ask whether this office of the apostles continues after their death: is there an "apostolic succession", or is their mission as one of a kind and unrepeatable as the earthly life, death and Resurrection of the Lord? Once again I can submit only a few brief remarks concerning this vehemently debated issue.

The first point I wish to make is that at the beginnings only the apostolic office itself stands before us with an altogether clearly delineated physiognomy, though it is admittedly Luke's theology that first completes the restriction of the title of apostle to the circle of the Twelve. Alongside the apostolate stand diverse kinds of offices, which, however, do not yet possess a permanently established form or fixed names and which undoubtedly also vary considerably depending on local situations. There are predominantly translocal ministries, such as that of the prophet and of the teacher. There are, in addition, locally exercised functions, which in the sphere of Jewish Christianity were designated by the term presbyter, probably a borrowing from synagogal government. For the domain of Gentile Christianity, on the other hand, we find "bishops and deacons" paired for the first time in the Letter to the Philippians (1:1). The theological clarification of the data under consideration matures slowly until it reaches its essential form in the phase leading up to the postapostolic period.

This process of clarification is mirrored in the New Testament in multiple ways. I would like to illustrate this process here in the light of just two texts that appear to me to be particularly important and illuminating. In this connection I am thinking first of Saint Paul's farewell discourse to the presbyters of Miletus, which

Luke has cast as the last will and testament of the apostle, who elsewhere also gathers the presbyters of Ephesus around himself for the same purpose. The text speaks of a formal instatement of successors: "Now be solicitous for yourselves and for the whole flock in which the Holy Ghost has appointed you as bishops to pasture the Church of God, which he purchased with his own blood" (Acts 20:28).

In this text the two terms *presbyter* and *episcopoi* are identified: the offices of Jewish and Gentile Christianity are equated and defined as a single office of apostolic succession. The text states that the Holy Spirit places men in this office: it is not a delegation on the part of the community, which for reasons of utility entrusts individuals with its communal functions, but the gift of the Lord, who gives personally what only he can give. As an office conferred by the Spirit, it is "sacramental". It is ultimately a continuation of the apostles' mission to feed God's flock. Hence, it takes up the pastoral ministry of Jesus Christ himself. Paul does not forget, of course, that Christ's pastorate culminates in the Cross: the good shepherd gives his life for his sheep. The structure of the apostolate leads back to the center of Christology. Thus, alongside of and prior to the identification of Jewish Christian and Gentile Christian ministries, alongside of the standardization of terminology, we can discover a second and more essential identification: the office of the presbyters and of the *episcopoi* is identical in its spiritual nature with that of the apostles.

Luke has even more precisely defined this identification, which secures the formulation of the principle of *successio apostolica*, by means of a further terminological option: by restricting the term apostle to the Twelve, he distinguishes what happened once only at the origin from what remains in perpetuity through succession. In this sense, the office of the presbyters and *episcopoi* is indeed something different from the apostolate of the Twelve. The presbyter-bishops are successors but are not themselves apostles. The "once only" as well as the "forever" belong to the structure of revelation and of the Church. The authority established by Christ to reconcile, pasture and teach continues unchanged in the successors, but they are apostles in the true sense only when and insofar as they "persevere in the teaching of the apostles" (Acts 2:42).

The same principles are formulated almost even more comprehensively and explicitly in the mirror for presbyters held up by the First Letter of Peter (5:1–4): "I admonish the presbyters among you as a fellow presbyter and witness of the sufferings of Christ as well as one who will have a share in the glory that is going to be revealed. Pasture the flock of God entrusted to you, not out of compulsion, but in conformity with God, freely, not out of avidity for gain, but out of voluntary dedication. Do not lord it over those committed to your care, but become an example for the flock. Then, when the supreme shepherd appears, you will receive in return an imperishable crown of glory." Right at the beginning of

this passage we find another significant process of identification: the apostle describes himself as copresbyter,
whereby he theologically identifies the apostolic office
and the presbyterate. The whole theology of apostleship
that we examined in the first part is thus applied to the
presbyterate, which creates a properly New Testament
theology of the priesthood. But this linking of the content of the two offices also ranks as a significant event
in the history of the Church: it is, so to say, the consummated act of *successio apostolica*, which also implicitly
establishes the idea of succession.

Yet another important theological process can be discerned in this brief text when it is read in the context
of the entire letter. Just as in the farewell discourse at
Miletus, here too the content of the mission of apostle and priest is summed up in the verb "pasture". It
is, in other words, defined in terms of the image of
the shepherd. But we must now add that Peter refers
to the Lord as "shepherd and bishop (ἐπίσκοπον) of
your souls" at the end of the second chapter (2:25) and
reverts once more to this point in our text where he
calls Christ the archshepherd (ἀρχιποιμήν). The formerly profane word *episkopos* is now identified with
the image of the shepherd and thus becomes a properly theological term, in which the nascent Church displays her distinctive new sacrality. If Peter connects the
priest with the apostle via the word copresbyter, he likewise links him via the word *episkopos*, meaning overseer or guardian, with *the episkopos*, Christ, the shepherd

himself, and in this way integrates all the elements in Christology.

On these grounds we can say in no uncertain terms that by the end of the apostolic era there is a full-blown theology of the priesthood of the New Covenant in the New Testament. This theology is given in trust to the Church and through the vicissitudes of history remains the basis of the inalienable identity of the priest.

### 3. Universal and particular priesthood— Old and New Testament

There still lies before us the question of how this new priestly office originating in the mission of Christ is related to the universal priesthood in the Church of the New Testament. There are two texts in the New Testament that speak of the universal priesthood: the ancient baptismal catechesis that is preserved for us in the First Letter of Peter and the salutation that John addresses to the seven communities at the beginning of the Book of Revelation (1 Pet 2:9; Rev 1:6). The formulas that are employed in both texts cite the words of God spoken to Israel in the Book of Exodus (19:6), when it is initiated into the covenant with God on Sinai and thereby receives the vocation to establish the right worship of God in the midst of the peoples who do not know him. As the chosen people, Israel has the mission to be the place of true adoration and thus to be at once priesthood and temple for the whole world.

When Christian baptismal catechesis applies to the baptized this word relating to the institution of the Old Covenant, it means that by baptism Christians enter upon the dignity of Israel—that baptism is the new Sinai. It signifies that the theology of Israel's election passes over to the Church as the new people of God. The Church as a whole must be God's dwelling in the world and the place where he is adored. Through the Church the world must be drawn into this adoration. Paul expresses this truth in the Letter to the Romans when he speaks of the grace granted to him "to be the minister [*leitourgos*] of Christ Jesus to the Gentile nations who ministers the gospel of God like a priest so that the Gentiles may become a sacrificial offering well-pleasing to God in the Holy Spirit" (Rom 15:16). The universal priesthood of the baptized, which follows from their entrance into God's covenant history inaugurated on Sinai, no more weighs against special priestly ministries than the common priesthood of Israel was opposed to its own priestly orders. At the same time, this principle allows us to discern clearly in what respect the ministerial office that is initiated in the Church with the apostles is something entirely new and in what respect it incorporates the preparatory forms of the Old Covenant in the very midst of its newness.

We can say quite straightforwardly that the Church's apostolic ministry is as new as Christ is; it partakes of the newness of Christ and proceeds from it. But just as Christ, who makes all things new and is God's new action in person, simultaneously recapitulates in himself all the promises that had oriented the whole of history toward him, in like manner the new priesthood of those sent by Jesus Christ also includes the entire prophetic content of the Old Covenant.

This emerges beautifully when we attend to the formula with which Jean Colson, drawing from a thorough analysis of the sources, has described the deepest essence of the Old Testament priesthood. He writes: "It is the chief function of the *kohanim* (ἱερεῖς) to keep the people aware of its priestly character and to work so that it might live in accordance with it, so that it might glorify God with its entire existence."[8] This statement is unmistakably close to the already-cited formula in which Paul speaks of his mission as *leitourgos* of Jesus Christ; the only difference is that the dynamic, missionary character of this expression now comes much more clearly to light as a consequence of the bursting open of the boundaries of Israel by the Cross of Christ. The ultimate end of all New Testament liturgy and of all priestly ministry is to make the world as a whole a temple and a sacrificial offering for God. This is to bring about the inclusion of the whole world into the

---

[8] J. Colson, *Ministre de Jésus-Christ ou le Sacerdoce de l'Évangile* (Paris, 1966), 185. Let me use this opportunity to draw the reader's attention to this fundamental study of biblical theology. The same view of the relationship between the two Testaments is corroborated and deepened by a careful exegesis of a single passage by G. Habets, "Vorbild und Zerrbild. Eine Exegese von Mal 1, 6–2, 9", in: *Teresianum* 41 (1990): 5–58.

Body of Christ, so that God may be all in all (cf. 1 Cor 15:28).

## 4. Conclusions for the priest of today

It is not now our intention to go on to a detailed consideration of the way in which all that we have said can be realized concretely today, particularly in the formation of priests.[9] In this context I would like to limit myself to a brief allusion to what seems to me to be of central importance.

We have seen that the New Testament priesthood inaugurated with the apostles has a thoroughly christological structure: it signifies the incorporation of man into the mission of Jesus Christ. Accordingly, the essential foundation of priestly ministry is a deep personal bond to Jesus Christ. Everything hinges on this bond, and the heart of all preparation for the priesthood and of all continuing priestly formation must be an introduction to it. The priest must be a man who knows Jesus intimately, who has encountered him and has learned to love him. For this reason the priest must be above all a man of prayer, a truly "spiritual" man. Without a strong spiritual substance, he cannot long endure in his ministry. Christ must also teach him that the main purpose

[9] Let me refer instead to my little study "Perspektiven der Priesterausbildung heute", in: J. Ratzinger, P. W. Scheele et al., *Unser Auftrag: Besinnungen auf den priesterlichen Dienst* (Würzburg, 1990), 11–38.

of his life is not self-realization and success. He must learn that he is not in the business of building himself an interesting or comfortable life, or of setting up for himself a community of admirers and devotees, but is working for another and that it is he who truly matters. This is initially opposed to the natural emphasis of our existence, but with time it proves that precisely this process in which the self becomes inconsequential is what truly liberates.

He who acts on Christ's behalf knows that it is always the case that one sows and another reaps. He does not need to bother incessantly about himself; he leaves the outcome to the Lord and does his own part without anxiety, free and cheerful because he is hidden within in the whole. If priests today so often feel overworked, tired and frustrated, the blame lies with a strained pursuit of results. Faith becomes a burdensome piece of baggage that the priest just barely manages to keep dragging along, whereas it should be a wing that bears us aloft.

Participation in Christ's love for men, in his will to save and help them, grows of itself out of intimate communion with him. Many priests today doubt whether it really benefits men to bring them to faith or whether one is not thereby making life harder for them. They think that it might be better to let men remain unbelievers in good conscience, because it seems easier to live that way. When faith is conceived merely as an added complication of life, it cannot give joy, nor can the service of the faith be a fulfilling task. But whoever has discovered Christ from inside and knows him firsthand also discovers that this relationship alone bestows meaning on everything else and transforms even difficulties into graces. Only such joy in Christ can also give joy for ministry and make it bear fruit.

He who loves desires to know. Therefore true love of Christ also expresses itself in the wish to know him ever better and to know everything that pertains to him. If love of Christ necessarily becomes love of men, it follows that education in Christ must include education in the natural virtues of humanity. If loving Christ implies getting to know him, it follows that the willingness to undertake committed and careful study is a sign of the seriousness of one's vocation and of the earnest inward search for intimacy with him. Training in faith is training in true humanity. It is also to learn the reason of faith. Because Christ is never alone but came in order to unite the world in his Body, love for the Church becomes an additional component: we do not seek a Christ whom we have invented, for only in the real communion of the Church do we encounter the real Christ. And once again the depth and seriousness of one's relation to the Lord himself is revealed in the ready willingness to love the Church, to live together with her and to serve Christ in her.

I would like to conclude by citing a text from Pope Saint Gregory the Great, in which he uses images of the Old Testament to describe the essential connection between interior life and ministry that we have men-

tioned here: "What else are holy men but rivers that
. . . water the parched earth? Yet they would . . . dry
up . . . if they . . . did not return to the place where
they began their course. That is, if they do not abide in
the interiority of the heart and do not bind themselves
fast with chains of longing in love for the Creator . . . ,
their tongue withers up. But out of love they constantly
return to this inner sanctuary, and what they . . . pour
out . . . in public they draw from the well . . . of love.
By loving they learn what they proclaim in teaching."[10]

---

[10] *In Ezechielem* 1, hom. 5, 16: PL 76, 828 B.

V

# A Company in Constant Renewal

*Preliminary remark*: This text was originally composed as a lecture for the annual "Meeting for Friendship among the Peoples" organized in Rimini by the movement "Comunione e Liberazione". The general theme of the meeting was defined by three symbolic figures—"*L'Ammiratore* (the wonderer)—Thomas Becket—Einstein", which explains why this text refers to them several times. The following topic had been formulated for my talk: "*Una compagnia sempre riformanda*" (a company in constant renewal), and the first section alludes to this deliberately vague title that I had been assigned.

## *1. Dissatisfaction with the Church*

It requires no great imagination to realize that the "company" about which I am going to speak here means the Church. The word Church was probably avoided in the title because it immediately provokes defensive reactions in the vast majority of people today. We have already heard, they say to themselves, all too much about the Church, and more often than not what we have heard has not been encouraging. The word Church and the reality it stands for have been discredited. It seems that even constant reform can hardly do much to change this situation. Or is it just that so far no one has discovered the kind of reform that could make of the Church a company worth belonging to?

But let us pause for a moment to ask a question: Why does the Church incur the dislike of so many men, even of believers, even of those who yesterday could be reckoned among the most faithful and who, despite their pain, probably still are today? The reasons are diverse, even contrary, depending on one's standpoint. Some are unhappy because the Church has conformed too much to the standards of the world; others are angry that she is still very far from doing so. Most people have trouble with the Church because she is an institution like many others, which as such restricts my freedom.

The thirst for freedom is the form in which the yearning for redemption and the feeling of unredemption and alienation make their voices heard today. The call for freedom demands an existence uncramped by prior givens that keep me from fully realizing myself and throw up external obstacles to my chosen path. But on all sides we run into such roadblocks that hold us at a standstill and prevent us from continuing on our way. The limits that the Church erects seem doubly burdensome because they reach into man's most personal and most intimate depths. For the Church's rules for ordering life are far more than a set of regulations to keep the shoulder-to-shoulder traffic of humanity as far as possible from collision. They inwardly affect my course in life, telling me how I am supposed to understand and shape my freedom. They demand of me decisions that cannot be made without painful renunciation. Is this not intended to deny us the sweetest fruits in the garden of life? Is not the way into the wide open closed by the restrictive confines of so many commandments and prohibitions? Is not thought kept from reaching its full stature just as much as the will is? Must not liberation consist in breaking out of such immature dependency? And would not the only real reform be to rid ourselves of the whole business? But what then still remains of this company?

Yet this bitterness against the Church has another more specific cause. For in the midst of a world full of harsh discipline and inexorable pressures, a secret hope still looks to the Church, which, it is felt, ought to be a kind of island of the good life, a tiny oasis of freedom into which one can withdraw now and then. Consequently, this rage at the Church, or disappointment with her, has a particular quality, because in their heart of hearts people expect more of her than of all worldly institutions. It is in the Church that the dream of a better world should be realized. There, at least, one would hope to know the taste of freedom, of redeemed existence—to emerge from the cave, as Gregory the Great expresses it in language borrowed from Plato.[1]

[1] Gregory the Great, *Hom. in Ex.* lib. 2, hom. 1, 17: PL 76, 948 A.

But because the Church as she appears empirically is so remote from such dreams, because she, too, smacks of institution and of everything human, an especially fierce anger wells up against her—an anger that nonetheless cannot part with the idea of the Church, because the dream that had turned men's eyes toward her in expectation cannot be extinguished. Because the Church is not as our dreams picture her to be, a desperate attempt is undertaken to bring her into conformity with our wishes: to make her a place for every freedom, a space where we can move freed of our limits, an experiment in utopia, which, after all, must exist somewhere. Just as our aim in politics is to introduce at long last a better world, we think that we must establish—perhaps as a first step toward the political goal—a better Church: a Church full of humanity, pervaded by a spirit of brotherhood and large-minded creativity, a place of reconciliation of all and for all.

### 2. Futile reform

But how is this to happen? How can such reform succeed? Well, the response is, we are just beginning. This is often said with the naive arrogance of the self-appointed enlightener who is convinced that previous generations did not get it right, or else were too fearful and unilluminated; we, on the other hand, supposedly now have the courage for the task and the understanding to go with it. However much reactionaries and "fundamentalists" may resist this noble project, it must be begun in earnest.

For the first step, at least, there is a thoroughly obvious recipe. The Church is not a democracy. She has not yet—so it seems—integrated into her constitution that basic patrimony of rights and freedoms elaborated by the Enlightenment that has since then been acknowledged as the basic rule for the political organization of communities. It thus appears as the most normal thing in the world to make up for lost time, which means first establishing once and for all this basic patrimony of structures of freedom. We must move—it is maintained—from the paternalistic Church to the community Church; no one must any longer remain a passive receiver of the gift of Christian existence. Rather, all should be active agents of it. The Church must no longer be fitted over us from above like a ready-made garment; no, we "make" the Church ourselves, and do so in constantly new ways. It thus finally becomes "our" Church, for which we are actively responsible. The passive yields to the active. The Church arises out of discussion, compromise and resolution. Debate brings out what can still be asked of people today, what can still be considered by common consent as faith or as ethical norms. New short formulas of faith are composed.

On a rather higher plane it has been said in Germany that even the liturgy ought no longer to conform to a prearranged pattern but in each case is the product of the community in which it is celebrated and develops in a given place and situation.[2] The liturgy itself must no longer be fixed in advance but must be something that we make in order to express what is unique about ourselves. This project finds something of an obstacle in the word of Scripture, which, however, cannot be dispensed with entirely. It must be handled quite selectively, and there are not a great many texts that can be utilized so as to fit smoothly into the self-realization that is now the apparent aim of the liturgy.

But questions immediately arise concerning this work

[2] This is the tenor, for example, of the following caption in the "Redaktionsbericht zum Einheitsgesangbuch" [Editorial report on the ecumenical hymnal] (Paderborn and Stuttgart, n. d.), edited by P. Nordhues and A. Wagner: "Das Meßformular ensteht am Ort" [The formulary of the Mass has local origins], 30. The subsequent elaboration of this point is considerably more measured; the "local" origins seem to be limited to the hymns of the proper. Why, then, this sensational title? According to a report in *Herderkorrespondenz*, the tendency that this title expresses was fully set forth at the 1990 conference of the "Arbeitsgemeinschaft katholischer Liturgiedozenten im deutschen Raum" [Seminar of Catholic teachers of liturgy in German-speaking countries]. The subject of "inculturation" was applied at the conference to the liturgy in the industrialized countries, in regard to which the question is said to be even less clear than for the developing nations. According to Hans Bernhard Meyer, at issue here is how "to discover forms of congregational worship that have arisen in present-day circumstances and at the same time are transparent to the mystery of God". He then claims that facts have begun to bear this out. "*The* Roman liturgy and *the* Roman missal at bottom already no longer exist today . . . , and this will be even truer in the future" (*Herderkorrespondenz* 44 [September 1990], 406). Liturgical scholarship that follows this course is in danger of negating itself.

of reform, which in place of all hierarchical tutelage will at long last introduce democratic self-determination into the Church. Who actually has the right to make decisions? What is the basis of the decision-making process? In a political democracy the answer to this question is the system of representation: individuals elect their representative, who makes decisions on their behalf. This commission has a time limit, its main lines of policy are clearly defined by the party system, and it embraces only those spheres of political action that are assigned to representative bodies by the constitution.

Questions remain even in regard to representation: the minority must submit to the majority, and this minority can be quite large. Furthermore, there is no infallible guarantee that my elected representative actually does act and speak as I wish. Once again, the victorious majority, seen from close up, can in no case consider itself entirely as the active subject of political events but must accept the decisions of others, at least in order not to jeopardize the system as a whole.

But there is a general question that is more relevant to our problem. Everything that men make can also be undone again by others. Everything that has its origin in human likes can be disliked by others. Everything that one majority decides upon can be revoked by another majority. A church based on human resolutions becomes a merely human church. It is reduced to the level of the makeable, of the obvious, of opinion. Opinion replaces faith. And in fact, in the self-made formulas of faith with which I am acquainted, the meaning of the words "I believe" never signifies anything beyond "we opine". Ultimately, the self-made church savors of the "self", which always has a bitter taste to the other self and just as soon reveals its petty insignificance. A self-made church is reduced to the empirical domain and thus, precisely as a dream, comes to nothing.

### 3. The essence of true reform

The maker is the opposite of the wonderer (*ammiratore*). He narrows the scope of reason and thus loses sight of the mystery. The more men themselves decide and do in the Church, the more cramped it becomes for us all. What is great and liberating about the Church is not something self-made but the gift that is given to us all. This gift is not the product of our own will and invention but precedes us and comes to meet us as the incomprehensible reality that is "greater than our heart" (cf. 1 Jn 3:20). The reform that is needed at all times does not consist in constantly remodelling "our" Church according to our taste, or in inventing her ourselves, but in ceaselessly clearing away our subsidiary constructions to let in the pure light that comes from above and that is also the dawning of pure freedom.

Let me express what I mean using a metaphor borrowed from Michelangelo, who in his turn is taking up ancient insights of Christian mysticism and philosophy.

With the eye of the artist, Michelangelo already saw in the stone that lay before him the pure image that, hidden within, was simply waiting to be uncovered. The artist's only task—so it seemed to him—was to remove what covered the statue.[3] Michelangelo considered the proper activity of the artist to be an act of uncovering, of releasing—not of making.

The same conception, applied to anthropology in general, is found in Saint Bonaventure, who explains the path by which man truly becomes himself with the help of the likeness of the sculptor. The sculptor, says the great Franciscan theologian, does not *make* anything, rather his work is *"ablatio"*—the removal of what is not really part of the sculpture. In this way, that is, by means of *ablatio*, the *nobilis forma*—the noble form—takes shape.[4] In the same way, continues Bonaventure,

---

[3] Cf. R. Cantalamessa, *Maria* (Milan, 1989), 127. To my joy I have learned that Chiara Lubich, the founder of the Focolare movement, dedicated a talk given at about the same time as my lecture in Rimini to the subject "L'arte del levare" (the art of removing) and in the course of this talk—in which she likewise referred to Michelangelo—developed ideas very similar to those that I attempt to set forth here.

[4] *Coll. in Hex.* 2, 33; Quaracchi ed., 5:342b. In Wilhelm Nyssen's translation (Bonaventura, *Das Sechstagewerk* [Munich, 1964], 139): "But this ascent takes place through affirmation (*affirmationem*) and removal. . . . Love always results from this removal. . . . Whoever makes a portrait (*sculpit figuram*) does not actually make anything and in the same stone leaves the noble and beautiful form (*relinquit formam nobilem et pulchram*). In this way the knowledge of the Godhead

man, in order that God's image may shine radiantly in him, must first and foremost receive the purification whereby the divine Sculptor frees him from that dross that conceals the authentic figure of his being, making him appear to be nothing more than a stone block, whereas the divine form dwells in him.

Rightly understood, this image contains the prototypical model of Church reform. The Church will constantly have need of human constructions to help her speak and act in the era in which she finds herself. Ecclesiastical institutions and juridical organizations are not intrinsically evil; on the contrary, to a certain degree they are simply necessary and indispensable. But they become obsolete; they risk setting themselves up as the essence of the Church and thus prevent us from seeing through to what is truly essential. This is why they must always be dismantled again, like scaffolding that has outlived its necessity. Reform is ever-renewed *ablatio*— removal, whose purpose is to allow the *nobilis forma*, the countenance of the bride, and with it the Bridegroom himself, the living Lord, to appear. Such *ablatio*, such "negative theology", is a path to something wholly positive. This path alone allows the divine to penetrate and brings about "*congregatio*", which as both gathering and purification is that pure communion we all long for,

---

through removal also leaves in us the clearest (better: the noblest— *nobilissimam*) form (*dispositionem!*).

where "I" is no longer pitted against "I" and self against self. Rather, the self-giving and self-abandonment that characterize love become the reciprocal reception of all that is good and pure. Thus, the word of the kindly father who reminds the jealous older son what the content of all freedom and the realization of utopia consist of becomes true for every man: "All that is mine is yours" (Lk 15:31; cf. Jn 17:10).

True reform, then, is *ablatio* (removal), which as such becomes *congregatio* (gathering). Let us attempt to formulate this fundamental idea somewhat more concretely. In our initial approach we had said that we were contrasting the wonderer (*ammiratore*) to the maker and were deciding for the former. But what is the meaning of this contrast? The maker values his own activity above all. He thereby restricts his horizon to the realm of things that he can grasp and that can become the object of his making. Strictly speaking, he sees only objects. He has absolutely no capacity to perceive what is greater than he is, since such a reality would set a limit to his activity. He squeezes the world into the empirical realm; man is amputated. Man builds himself his own prison, against which he then noisily protests. True wonder, on the other hand, is a No to this confinement in empirical, this-worldly reality. It prepares man for the act of faith, which opens to him the horizon of the eternal and infinite. And only the unlimited is large enough for our nature and in accord with the call of our essential being. When this horizon disappears, every remaining freedom becomes too small, and all the liberations that may then be offered are a vapid substitute that never equals what has been lost. The primary, the fundamental *ablatio* that is needed for the Church is the act of faith itself, which breaks the barriers of finitude and thus creates the open space that reaches into the unlimited. Faith leads us into the "broad places", as the Psalms put it (for example, Ps 31 [30]:9).

Modern scientific thought has increasingly shut us up in the prison of positivism, thus condemning us to pragmatism. Much can be achieved by doing so; it is possible to journey to the moon and still farther into the immensity of the universe. Yet in spite of this, man always remains in the same place, because he does not surpass the real limit, which is set by what can be quantified and produced. Albert Camus has portrayed the absurdity of this freedom in the character of the emperor Caligula: everything is at his disposal, and everything is too little for him. In his insane craving for more, for something bigger, he cries: "I want the moon, give me the moon!"[5] By now it is more or less possible to have the moon, but when the real boundary—the boundary between earth and heaven, between God and the world —does not open, even the moon is merely an additional piece of earth, and by reaching it man is not brought

---

[5] *Caligula*, act 1, scene 4, in: A. Camus, *Théâtre. Récits Nouvelles*, Bibliothèque de la Pléiade (Paris, 1962), 15ff. For an interpretation, see G. Linde, *Das Problem der Gottesvorstellungen im Werk von A. Camus* (Münster, 1975), 31.

one step closer to the freedom and plenitude he longs for.

The fundamental liberation that the Church can give us is to permit us to stand in the horizon of the eternal and to break out of the limits of our knowledge and capabilities. In every age, therefore, faith itself in its full magnitude and breadth is the essential reform that we need; it is in the light of faith that we must test the value of self-constructed organizations in the Church. This implies that the Church must be the bridge of faith and must not—especially in her life as an inner-worldly association—become an end in herself. Nowadays the opinion surfaces occasionally even in ecclesiastical circles that a man is more Christian the more he is involved in Church activities. We have a kind of ecclesiastical occupational therapy; a committee, or at any rate some sort of activity in the Church, is sought for everyone. People—according to this way of thinking—must constantly be busy about the Church, they must always be talking about the Church, or doing something to or in her. But a mirror that reflects only itself is no longer a mirror; a window that no longer lets us see the wide open spaces outside, but gets in the way of the view, has lost its reason for being.

There can be people who are engaged uninterruptedly in the activities of Church associations and yet are not Christians. There can be people who simply live by word and sacrament alone and practice the love born of faith without ever having attended Church groups,

without ever having concerned themselves with the
novelties of ecclesiastical politics, without having taken
part in synods and voted in them—and yet are true
Christians. We need, not a more human, but a more
divine Church; then she will also become truly human.
And for this reason everything man-made in the Church
must recognize its own purely ancillary character and
leave the foreground to what truly matters.

The freedom that we rightly expect from and in the
Church is not achieved by introducing the principle of
majority. This freedom does not rest on the fact that as
many as possible prevail against as few as possible. Its
basis is rather that no one may impose his own will on
the others, since all know themselves to be bound to
the word and will of the One who is our Lord and our
freedom.

In the Church the atmosphere becomes cramped and
stifling when her officebearers forget that the sacrament
is, not an allocation of power, but dispossession of myself for the sake of the one in whose "persona" I am to
speak and act. But when ever-greater self-dispossession
matches ever-greater responsibility, no one is the servant
of another; there the Lord rules, and there it proves true
that: "The Lord is the Spirit. But where the Spirit of
the Lord is, there is freedom" (2 Cor 3:17). The more
administrative machinery we construct, be it the most
modern, the less place there is for the Spirit, the less place
there is for the Lord, and the less freedom there is.

It is my opinion that we ought to begin an unsparing

examination of conscience on this point at all levels in the Church. On every level this would have to have very real consequences and would be bound to bring about an *ablatio* that would allow the true inherent form to reemerge and could restore to us in a wholly new way the feeling of freedom and of being at home.

### 4. Morality, forgiveness and expiation— the personal center of reform

Before we proceed further, let us look back for a moment on our considerations up to this point. We have spoken of a double "removal" (*ablatio*)—of a double act of liberation, which is a double act of purification and renewal. The first point of discussion was faith, which breaches the wall of finitude and opens up an unobstructed view into the broad spaces of eternity— not only the view, but also the way. For faith is not just cognition but action; it is not only a cleft in the wall but the saving hand that leads us forth out of the cave. We had drawn the conclusion that this implies for institutions: the essential basis of Church order constantly needs to be developed and applied concretely so that the Church's life can unfold in a particular period; but what we create for this purpose must never take the place of what is the heart of the matter. For the Church, unlike an inner-worldly association, does not exist in order to keep us busy and to support *herself* but in order to break free into eternal life in all of us.

We must now make a further step and transpose the whole of this from the general and objective to the personal. For here, too, there is need of liberating "removal". Indeed, it is hardly the case that we always and immediately see in the other the "noble form", the image of God that is inscribed in him. What first meets the eye is only the image of Adam, the image of man, who, though not totally corrupt, is nonetheless fallen. We see the crust of dust and filth that has overlaid the image. Thus, we all stand in need of the true sculptor who removes what distorts the image; we are in need of forgiveness, which is the heart of all true reform.

It is certainly no accident that the forgiveness of sins plays an essential role in the three decisive stages of the birth of the Church that the Gospels recount to us. The first episode is the consignment of the keys to Peter. The bestowal of the power to bind and to loose, to open and to shut, which the Gospel speaks of here is in its core an authority to let in, to bring home, to forgive (Mt 16:19).[6] We find the same reality again at the Last Supper, which inaugurates the new communion from and in the Body of Christ. This communion is made

[6] J. Gnilka, *Das Matthäusevangelium* (Freiburg im Breisgau, 1988), 2:65: "But by rejecting the Gospel, they (the doctors of the law) close . . . the reign of heaven to men. Simon Peter takes their place. If one considers this contrast attentively, it turns out that the chief task assigned to the disciple's competence is to open the reign of heaven. His task must be characterized as positive." Even if the power to forgive sins is not regarded as the primary meaning of the logion about binding and loosing, this power cannot be detached from it.

possible by the Lord's shedding his blood "for many for the forgiveness of sins" (Mt 26:28). Finally, the risen Lord establishes the communion of his peace when he first appears to the Eleven. He does so by giving them full authority to forgive (Jn 20:19–23). The Church is not a communion of those "who have no need of the physician" (Mk 2:17) but a communion of converted sinners who live by the grace of forgiveness and transmit it themselves.

When we read the New Testament attentively, we discover that there is nothing magical about forgiveness. But neither is it a fictitious forgetting, a refusal to accept the truth, but an entirely real process of change carried out by the Sculptor. The removal of guilt truly *gets rid* of something; the proof that forgiveness has come in us is that penance springs up from us. Forgiveness is in this sense an active-passive event: the creative word of power that God speaks to us produces the pain of conversion and thus becomes an active self-transformation. Forgiveness and penance, grace and personal conversion are not contradictions but two sides of one and the same event. This fusion of activity and passivity expresses the essential form of human existence, for all of our creativity begins with our having been created, with our participation in God's creative activity.

Here we have reached a very central point: I believe that the core of the spiritual crisis of our time has its basis in the obscuration of the grace of forgiveness. But let us first take note of the positive side of the present:

morality is gradually coming back into favor. It is recognized, indeed, it has become evident, that all technical progress is questionable and, in the end, destructive when there is no corresponding moral advancement. It is recognized that there is no reform of man or of humanity without moral renewal. But the call for morality ultimately remains without effect, because the criteria are veiled in a fog of discussions. In fact, man cannot bear sheer morality, he cannot live by it: it becomes a "law" for him that provokes contradiction and engenders sin. For this reason, where forgiveness—true forgiveness guaranteed by authority—is not recognized or believed, morality must be cut down to size so that the conditions of sinful action can never actually occur for the individual. Today's discussion of morality is making great strides toward liberating man from guilt by precluding the occurrence of the conditions that make it possible. One is reminded of the mordant aphorism of Pascal: "Ecce patres qui tollunt peccata mundi!" (Behold the fathers who take away the sins of the world). According to these "moralists", guilt simply no longer exists.

It goes without saying, however, that this method of freeing the world from guilt is all too cheap. In their heart of hearts, those who have been liberated in this fashion know perfectly well that the whole experience is untrue; they know that there is sin, that they themselves are sinners and that there must be a real way to overcome sin.[7] Nor indeed does Jesus call those who have already freed themselves and who therefore—as they think—have no need for him whatever; rather, he calls those who know themselves to be sinners and for this very reason are in need of him. Morality retains its seriousness only where there is forgiveness—real forgiveness ensured by authority; otherwise it lapses back into the pure empty conditional. But true forgiveness exists only when the "price", the "equivalent value", is paid, when guilt is atoned by suffering, when there is expiation. The circular link between morality, forgiveness and expiation cannot be forced apart at any point; when one element is missing, everything else is ruined. Whether or not man can find redemption depends on the undivided existence of this circle. In the Torah, the five books of Moses, these three elements are knotted

[7] See on this point the remarkable essay of A. Görres, "Schuld und Schuldgefühle", in: *Internationale katholische Zeitschrift* 13 (1984): 430–43: "Psychoanalysis has found it difficult to admit that among other guilt feelings there are also some that can be traced back to real guilt. It cannot accept these data without embarrassment . . . because its philosophy does not recognize freedom . . . its determinism is the opium of the intellectuals. In the psychoanalytic mind, Sigmund Freud far surpassed the poor unenlightened Rabbi Jesus. He, in fact, could only forgive sins and still found it necessary to do so, whereas Sigmund Freud, the new Messiah from Vienna, did far more: he rid the intellectual world of sin and guilt" (438). "In the household economy of the soul, feelings of guilt are . . . necessary, indispensable . . . for psychic health. Thus, anyone who is so cool that he no longer experiences feelings of guilt where they are appropriate ought to try with all his might to recover them" (433f.).

together inseparably, and it is therefore impossible to follow the Enlightenment in excising from this core of the Old Testament canon an eternally valid moral law, while consigning the rest to past history. This moralistic manner of giving the Old Testament relevance for today is bound to fail; it was already the pith of the heresy of Pelagius, who has more followers today than appears at first glance.

Jesus, on the other hand, fulfilled the *whole* law, not a portion of it, and thus renewed it from the ground up: he himself, who suffered the whole tale of guilt, is at once expiation and forgiveness and is therefore also the only reliable and perennially valid basis of our morality. It is impossible to detach morality from Christology, because it is impossible to separate it from expiation and forgiveness.

In Christ, the whole law is fulfilled, and morality has thereby become a more concrete claim on us that it is now more possible to satisfy. From the core of faith, then, the way of renewal opens again and again for the individual, for the Church as a whole and for humanity.

## 5. Pain, martyrdom and the joy of redemption

There would be much to say about this. But I shall merely attempt in conclusion to outline very briefly what seems to me to be the most crucial point in this context. Forgiveness, together with its realization in me by way of penance and discipleship, is first of all the wholly personal center of all renewal. But because forgiveness touches the very core of the person, it gathers men together and is also the center of the renewal of the community. For when the dust and filth that disfigure God's image in me are removed, I thereby become similar to the other who is likewise God's image; above all I become similar to Christ, who is the image of God without qualification, the model according to which we have all been created.

Paul expresses this happening in quite drastic terms: the old image sinks into nothingness, a new being has arisen (2 Cor 5:17)—it is no longer I who live but Christ who lives in me (Gal 2:20). What Paul is describing is an event of birth and death. I am wrested from my isolation and incorporated into the communion of a new subject; my "I" is inserted into the "I" of Christ and consequently joined to the "I" of all my brothers. Only from such deep renewal of the individual does Church come into being as a communion that binds us together and sustains us in life and death. Only if we think this entirely through do we see the Church in the right order of magnitude.

The Church is not only the small group of activists who come together in a given place in order to set parish life in motion. Nor is the Church merely the crowd of those who meet on Sunday to celebrate the Eucharist. Finally, the Church is also more than the pope, bishops and priests, the holders of sacramental office. All those whom we have mentioned belong to the Church, but the radius of the "company" (*compagnia*) into which we enter by faith reaches farther—beyond the limits of death.

To her belong all the saints: from Abel and Abraham and all the witnesses of hope of whom the Old Testament tells us, through Mary, the Mother of the Lord, and the Lord's apostles, through Thomas Becket and Thomas More all the way to Maximilian Kolbe, Edith Stein, and Pier Giorgio Frassati. The Church includes all the unknown and unnamed "whose faith is known to him alone";[8] she embraces the men of all places and all times whose hearts stretch out in hope and love to Christ, the "author and finisher of faith", as the Letter to the Hebrews calls him (12:2).

The fortuitous majorities that may form here or there in the Church do not decide their and our path: they, the saints, are the true, the normative majority by which we orient ourselves.[9] Let us adhere to them; they translate the divine into the human, eternity into time; they teach us what it is to be human, and they never abandon even

[8] From the *memento mortuorum* of the fourth Eucharistic Prayer.

[9] See on this point Cardinal J. Meisner, *Wider die Entsinnlichung des Glaubens* (Graz, 1990), 35: "Democracy in the Church means to accord the right to be heard in the present-day generation of Christians to the generations who have believed, hoped, loved and suffered before us." In fact majority in the Church can never exist only synchronically but in essence is always purely diachronic, because the saints of all times are alive and because they are the true Church.

us in our pain and solitude; indeed, they accompany us at the hour of our death.

Here we touch upon a very important point. A world-view that is incapable of giving even pain meaning and value is good for nothing. It falls short precisely at the hour of the most serious crisis of existence. Those who have nothing to say about suffering except that we must fight against it are deceiving us. It is, of course, necessary to do everything one can to lessen the suffering of the innocent and to limit pain. But there is no human life without suffering, and he who is incapable of accepting suffering is refusing himself the purifications that alone allow us to reach maturity. In communion with Christ, pain becomes meaningful, not only for myself, as a process of *ablatio* in which God purges me of the dross that conceals his image, but beyond me, for the whole, so that we can all say with Saint Paul: "But now I rejoice in my sufferings for you and so complete in my flesh what is still lacking in the afflictions of Christ for the sake of his body, the Church" (Col 1:24).

Thomas Becket, who together with the figure of the wonderer (*ammiratore*) and with that of Einstein, has stood in the background of our reflections, encourages us onward to a final step. Life reaches farther than our biological existence. Where there is no longer anything worth dying for, even life itself is no longer worth living. When faith has opened our eyes and has enlarged our heart, yet another word of Saint Paul attains its full illuminating power: "None of us lives for himself, and no one dies for himself. If we live, we live for the Lord; if we die, we die for the Lord; whether we live or die, we are the Lord's'' (Rom 14:7f.). The more we are rooted in this company with Jesus Christ and with all who belong to him, the more our life will be sustained by that radiant confidence that Saint Paul has once again put into words: "Of this I am sure: neither life nor death, neither angels nor powers, neither things present nor things to come, no authorities, neither height nor depth nor any creature at all can separate us from the love of God that is in Christ Jesus our Lord" (Rom 8:38f.).

We must allow ourselves to be filled with such faith. It is then that the Church will grow as a company into true life and renew herself from day to day. It is then that she will become a spacious house with many mansions; it is then that the multiplicity of the gifts of the Spirit will be free to operate in her. It is then that we shall behold "how good and pleasant it is for brethren to dwell in unity. . . . It is like the dew of Hermon that falls upon Mount Zion; for there the Lord grants blessing and life forever" (Ps 133:1, 3).

# Epilogue:

# Party of Christ or
# Church of Jesus Christ?

*Homily for the Third Sunday in Ordinary Time*
*(lectionary year A)*

The reading we have just heard from Saint Paul's First
Letter to the Corinthians is almost disconcertingly up-
to-date. Paul is speaking, of course, with the Corinthian
community of the time and is trying to awaken its conscience to see all the ways in which it contradicts true
Christian existence. But we immediately realize that
this reading is not only about the problems of a Christian community of the distant past but that what Paul
wrote then captures our own situation here and now.
As he speaks to the Corinthians, Paul is speaking to
us, and he puts his finger on the wounds of our life
as Church today. Like the Corinthians, we too run the
risk of fragmenting the Church into a factional strife in
which every contestant develops his own idea of Christianity. In this way the rightness of one's own position
becomes more important than God's claim on us, than
being right before him. Our own idea conceals from
us the word of the living God, and the Church disappears behind the parties that grow out of our per-

sonal opinion. The similarity between the situation of
the Corinthians and ours cannot be missed. But Paul
does not intend simply to describe a situation; rather,
he speaks to us in order to rouse our conscience and to
guide us back to the true totality and unity of Christian
existence.

We must ask him, then: Just what is it that is false
about our attitude? What must we do in order to become, not the party of Paul or of Apollo or of Cephas or
even a party of Christ, but the Church of Jesus Christ?
What is the difference between a party of Christ and
his living Church? Between a party of Cephas and the
right fidelity to the rock upon which the house of the
Lord is built?

Accordingly, let us first attempt to understand what
is actually taking place in Corinth and which constantly
threatens to repeat itself anew in history because of the
ever-recurring temptations to which man is exposed.
We could perhaps briefly sum up the distinction that is
meant here in the following statement: When I advocate a party, it thereby becomes *my* party, whereas the
Church of Jesus Christ is never *my* Church but always
*his* Church. Indeed, the essence of conversion lies precisely in the fact that I cease to pursue a party of my
own that safeguards my interests and conforms to my
taste but that I put myself in his hands and become his,
a member of his Body, the Church.

Let us try to elucidate this point in somewhat greater
detail still. The Corinthians see in Christianity an in-

teresting religious theory that answers to their taste
and their expectations. They choose what suits them,
and they select it in the form that pleases them. But
when one's own will and desire is the decisive criterion, schism is a foregone conclusion, because there are
multiple and opposing varieties of taste. A club, a circle
of friends, a party can grow from such an ideological
choice, but not a Church that overcomes antitheses between men and unites them in the peace of God. The
principle by which a club develops is personal taste; but
the principle on which the Church is based is obedience to the call of the Lord as we see it in the Gospel:
"He called them, and immediately they left the boat
and their father and followed Jesus" (Mt 4:21f.).

This brings us to the crucial point. Faith is not the
selection of a program that is to my liking or the join-
ing of a club of friends in which I feel understood but
is a conversion that transforms me and my taste along
with it, or at least makes my taste and my wishes take
second place. Faith penetrates to an entirely different
depth than can be attained by a choice that pledges me
to a party. Its power to change is so far-reaching that
Scripture designates it as a new birth (cf. 1 Pet 1:3, 23).

We find ourselves before an important insight that we
must continue to deepen somewhat further, inasmuch
as it touches upon the hidden heart of the problems
with which we are occupied in the Church today. It
is difficult for us to conceive of the Church otherwise
than according to the model of a self-governing soci-

ety that attempts to organize itself in a way that is acceptable to all its members by mechanisms of majority and minority. We have difficulty understanding faith otherwise than as a decision for a cause that I like and to which I therefore wish to lend my support. But in all this we ourselves remain the sole actors. *We* make the Church, we try to improve her and to arrange her like a comfortable house. *We* want to offer programs and ideas that appeal to as many as possible. That God himself becomes active, that *he* acts is something that we no longer take for granted in the modern world. But precisely by making this assumption, we follow in the footsteps of the Corinthians: we confuse the Church with a party and faith with a party program. The circle of what *we* do and are remains closed.

Perhaps we are now a little better able to comprehend what a turnabout faith entails—to grasp the re-versal, the con-version that it contains: I acknowledge that God himself speaks and acts; I recognize the existence not only of what is ours but also of what is his. But if this is true, if we are not the only ones who choose and act, but he too speaks and acts, then everything changes. Then I must obey, then I must follow him, even when he leads me where I do not wish to go (Jn 21:18). Then it becomes reasonable, indeed, necessary, to let go of my own taste, to renounce my own wishes and to follow after him who alone can show the way to true life, because he himself is the life (Jn 14:6). This is what Paul means by the cruciform character of discipleship, which he underlines at the conclusion of the reading as the answer to the Corinthian party system (10:17): I abandon *my* taste and submit myself to *him*. But it is in this very way that I am set free, because the real slavery is imprisonment in the circle of our own wishes.

We understand all of this even better when we regard it from the other side, not from our point of view, but from that of the acting God himself. Christ is not the founder of a party and not a religious philosopher, a fact to which Paul emphatically draws attention in our reading (1 Cor 10:17). He is not someone who thinks up for himself all sorts of ideas and recruits adherents to them.

The Letter to the Hebrews characterizes the entrance of Christ into the earthly world with the words of Psalm 40: Sacrifice and oblation you desired not; you have prepared for me a body (Ps 40:7; Heb 10:5). Christ is God's very living word who has become flesh for our sake. He is not only one who speaks, he himself is his own word. His love, in which God gives himself to us, goes to the very end, to the Cross (cf. Jn 13:1). When we say Yes to him, we do not merely choose ideas but put our life in his hands and become a "new creation" (2 Cor 5:17; Gal 6:15).

This is why the Church is not a club, not a party, not even a sort of religious state within the secular state, but a body—Christ's Body. And this is why the Church is not of our making but is constructed by the Lord himself when he cleanses us by Word and sacrament and thus makes us his members. There is, of course, a great deal that we ourselves must organize in the Church, because she is deeply immersed in very practical human matters. It is not my intention to support any false supernaturalism here. But what truly makes the Church the Church cannot come from our own willing and deciding; it cannot come "from the will of the flesh or from the will of man" (Jn 1:13); it must be from him. The more we ourselves do in the Church, the more uninhabitable she becomes, because everything human is limited and is in opposition to other human realities. The Church will be all the more the homeland for man's heart, the more we listen to God and the more what comes from him is of central importance in her: his Word and the sacraments he has given us. The obedience of all toward him is the guarantee of our freedom.

All of this has very important consequences for priestly ministry. The priest must attend carefully lest he build his own Church. Paul himself examines his conscience downright anxiously: How could people go so far as to create a Pauline religious party out of the Church of Christ? He assures himself and, therefore, the Corinthians as well, that he has done everything in his power to avoid attachments that might obstruct communion with Christ. He who converts under Paul's influence does not become an adherent of Paul but a Christian, a member of the one Church common to all, which is ever the same "whether Paul, or Apollo or Cephas" (1 Cor 3:22). Whether the former or the latter: "You are Christ's and Christ is God's" (3:23). It is worth the effort to reread the whole passage and to examine meticulously what Paul has written on this point, because it brings to light the essential core of the priestly office with a clarity that surpasses every theory and tells us in practical terms what we have to do and not do. "What is Apollo, what is Paul? Servants, through whom you have believed. . . . I have planted, Apollo has watered, but God has given the increase. Neither the one who plants nor the one who waters is anything—but rather the one who gives the increase: God. He who plants and he who waters are one . . . we are coworkers of God; you are God's field, God's building" (1 Cor 3:5–9).

In Protestant Churches in Germany, there was and is the custom of announcing on the bulletin board who is celebrating the service and preaching the homily. Such names often stand for religious parties: everyone wants to attend the service of his own camp. Unfortunately a similar use is now beginning in Catholic parishes; but this means that the Church is disappearing behind parties, that ultimately we are listening to human opinions and no longer heeding the common Word of God that transcends us all and whose guarantor is the Church. Only the unity of the Church's faith and her authority, which is binding on each member, assures us that we are not following human opinions and adhering to self-made party groupings but that we belong to the Lord and are obeying him.

There is a great danger today that the Church will disintegrate into religious parties that rally around individual teachers or preachers. And if this is so, what was true then is true once more: I am Apollo's, I am Paul's, I am Cephas', and we end by making even Christ into a party. The norm of priestly ministry is the selflessness that submits itself to the measure of Jesus' word: "My doctrine is not mine" (Jn 7:16). Only when we can say this in all truth are we "coworkers of God" who plant and water and thus become partakers of his own work. When men appeal to us and oppose our Christianity to that of others, this must always be a motive for us to examine our conscience. We proclaim, not ourselves, but him. This requires our humility, the cross of discipleship. But it is precisely this that frees us, that enriches and enlarges our ministry. For when we proclaim ourselves, we remain ensconced in our miserable "I" and draw others in to share our billet. When we preach him, we become "coworkers of God" (1 Cor 3:9), and what could be more magnificent and more liberating than that?

Let us ask the Lord to give us a renewed perception of the joy of this mission. When he does, the word of the prophet will once again prove true in our midst as well. This is the word that is always fulfilled when Christ walks among the nations: The people who live in darkness have seen a great light. . . . We rejoice in your nearness, just as they rejoice at the harvest, as they shout for joy when they divide the spoils (Is 9:1–2; cf. Mt 4:16). Amen.